P9-CMY-504

Confession
Finding Freedom and Forgiveness

FR. PAUL FARREN
FOREWORD BY JEAN VANIER

PARACLETE PRESS
BREWSTER, MASSACHUSETTS

2014 First Printing This Edition

Confession: Finding Freedom and Forgiveness

Copyright © 2014 by Paul Farren

ISBN 978-1-61261-522-6

First edition, 2013, published by The Columba Press, 55A Spruce Avenue, Stillorgan Industrial Park, Blackrock, Co. Dublin.

The Paraclete Press name and logo (dove on cross) is a trademark of Paraclete Press, Inc.

Library of Congress Cataloging-in-Publication Data is available.

10 9 8 7 6 5 4 3 2 1

All rights reserved. No portion of this book may be reproduced, stored in an electronic retrieval system, or transmitted in any form or by any means—electronic, mechanical, photocopy, recording, or any other—except for brief quotations in printed reviews, without the prior permission of the publisher.

Published by Paraclete Press
Brewster, Massachusetts
www.paracletepress.com
Printed in the United States of America

I dedicate this book to the memory of my mother.

CONTENTS

ACKNOWLEDGMENTS

I thank The Columba Press for publishing the first edition of this book.

The book was long in coming! In truth it began back in 1997 in the Catholic University of America in Washington, DC. There Sr. Catherine Dooley, OP, encouraged me to study the sacrament of Reconciliation. Through her enthusiasm I have developed a great love for the sacrament. I want to thank Sr. Kate for her guidance and her friendship and for helping me with this book.

I thank my colleagues at the Derry Diocesan Catechetical Centre, who have supported me so much in this work. I also thank all those who read the book and made comments and corrections. They are greatly appreciated.

I thank Jean Vanier for his wisdom, advice and encouragement during the writing of this book and I thank him for writing the foreword.

The sacrament of Reconciliation can be talked about endlessly but for it to be alive it needs to be celebrated. I am so grateful for the accompaniment I have in celebrating the sacrament that makes it such a joyful experience and for all the priests who have confessed God's forgiveness for me.

My greatest thanks go to my family. I thank my father and my mother, my sister, Marie, her husband Noel and their children Emmet, Kate and Eoghan, who have taught me so much about love and forgiveness. I pray in thanksgiving for the gift of my mother and trust that she is now in the peace and joy of heaven.

FOREWORD

JEAN VANIER

FATHER PAUL FARREN CAME TO SEE ME IN 1992 in Trosly-Breuil, France, where I had created the first community of l'Arche in 1964. He came to see the community. A number of years later he invited me to give a retreat in Derry. He had heard about the meaning of l'Arche and how people with disabilities in our communities were able to develop humanly and spiritually because they felt loved, appreciated and understood. As we shared together we realized that what is true for people with disabilities is true for every person, for every Christian: they can only grow spiritually and deepen in their faith as they become conscious that they are loved, appreciated and understood by Jesus.

Of course, at l'Arche there are laws and regulations which we all have to obey; but our fundamental happiness and our desire to grow flow from the love we encounter. So it is for every Christian: laws and regulations are necessary, but we accept and live these laws because of a personal relationship with Jesus who is calling us to become his friend. This friendship is celebrated in the sacraments. There is an intimate relationship between the sacrament of Communion in the Eucharist and the sacrament of Reconciliation.

Somewhere along the line in the history of the Church, people have become more centered upon obedience to laws than upon this relationship of love with a person, with Jesus; more centered upon justice than upon love. The heart of our faith is not law, it is a person, Jesus, who calls us into the peace and joy of friendship and of love.

I have had the pleasure to be with Paul many times over the years, in the North of Ireland and in Trosly. We have been able to share about the Church in this period of history, about the joy and pain of priesthood, about the call of lay people to a friendship with Jesus. I have sensed the deep love of Paul for his priesthood, for the Church and for the people he is called to serve and to lead as a good shepherd.

We have shared many times about the beauty of the sacrament of Reconciliation and how it has tended to become the forgotten sacrament, wondering is this because it has been seen more as a sort of tribunal rather than as an encounter of friendship.

We can understand forgiveness when we think of an angry dispute between a father and a son, a husband and a wife, which ends up with one slamming the door and going away. Forgiveness is when the one who ran away comes back and says, "I am sorry." Forgiveness then is a celebration of love and of communion.

This excellent little book, written by a priest who has spent much time hearing Confessions, and has seen not only its beauty but also how it can become a sterile ritual, flows from the understanding of Confession as a meeting of love and as a renewal of friendship. Confession can become, then, a beautiful way to grow in love and to be more deeply inspired by the Spirit of Jesus, given to us all at baptism.

INTRODUCTION

She was about the one age with Gran; she was well-to-do, lived in a big house on the Montenotte, wore a black cloak and bonnet, and came every day to school at three o'clock when we should have been going home, and talked to us of hell. She may have mentioned the other place as well, but that could only have been by accident, for hell had the first place in her heart.

(Frank O'Connor, My First Confession*)*

BETWEEN HISTORY AND FOLKLORE, THE STORY OF the sacrament of Confession seems to have been inextricably linked with hell. For this reason there was much fear and even, perhaps, superstition associated with the sacrament. Many people went to Confession simply to avoid going to hell were they to die suddenly. Priests in their sermons often increased the fear of the people by reiterating the connection between Confession and hell. I am told that there was a priest in my home parish years ago who had a great ability to mutter. Nobody could hear much of what he was saying, however, every so often he would raise his voice and shout, "You are all going to hell!"

Fear can be a powerful controlling mechanism. In the past, fear of hell was probably what motivated many to confess regularly and frequently. Was going to Confession no more than strict adherence to a law of the Church?

Over the last forty years there has been a dramatic change in the practice of Confession. Today it is probably the most talked about and yet the least celebrated sacrament of the Catholic Church. Some people have declared the death of the sacrament saying that it belongs to a different era and a different time. Others bemoan the fact that the same emphasis is not being placed on hell today, perhaps believing that a bit of fear is good and healthy and should be reclaimed. In the midst of all this discussion and debate, questions beg to be asked: does the sacrament have a future and, if it does, what is that future?

To answer these questions the sacrament of Reconciliation needs to be considered in the context of our relationship with God, with ourselves, with the Church, and in the world. However, in order to do this we need firstly to look to the past and consider how the sacrament evolved. It would be wrong to think that the sacrament of Reconciliation has remained the same down through history. In fact, it has had a long and complicated history.

THE TIME OF THE APOSTLES

The sacrament evolved from the earliest times when members of the new church tried to deal with people who committed sin after their Baptism. At the time of the Apostles, Baptism was understood as being reborn or dying to one's old self and rising with Christ (John 3:1–15 & Rom. 6:1–12). It was the sacrament of forgiveness.

If someone sinned after Baptism, forgiveness and reconciliation were obtained through prayer, fasting, almsgiving, and works of mercy. The prayer was of the individual but also of the community, which, it was believed, could bring healing (Jas. 5:16). Some communities did not think that prayer was appropriate for certain sins (1 John 5:14–17). If the person's sins were public or scandalous, exclusion from the life of the community for some period of time was necessary. The community had the authority to impose this exclusion (Mt. 18:17 & 1 Cor. 5:3–5). The exclusion was because the sin was an offense against God and "a contradiction to membership in the Church and a denial of the very nature of Church."[1]

Through this exclusion a person's sin was recognized and after a period of conversion, which involved penance, they were reconciled with the community again.

CANONICAL PENANCE

This process became very formal over the early centuries of the Church and was known as a "second Baptism" because it was a once in a lifetime opportunity for sinners excluded from communion to be reconciled with the Church. This meant entering the order of

---

1. Catherine Dooley, "The Role of the Community in the Sacrament of Reconciliation," *Louvain Studies 14* (1989): 315.

penitents, which was a group of sinners who wanted back into communion with the Church. The penitent was a member of this order for a prescribed period of time, during which he/she underwent a conversion process, supported by prayer, rites, severe penances, acts of service, and making amends where necessary. This process was called Canonical Penance. The period of Canonical Penance came to an end in Lent, the designated period of final preparation for reconciliation and for the return to the Eucharistic table. A liturgy of reconciliation took place on Holy Thursday presided over by the bishop. During this liturgy the bishop laid hands on the sinners, who were known as penitents, as a gesture of reconciliation. After the liturgy those who were reconciled got ready for full participation in the Easter celebrations.

Through time this practice began to dissolve due mainly to the severity of the penance and the long-term exclusion from the sacraments that often took place. However, from about the fifth century in Rome many people chose to become "ceremonial penitents for the duration of Lent"[2] and by the tenth century all Christians were expected to become ceremonial penitents for Lent.

---

2. James Dallen, "Sacrament of Reconciliation," in *The New Dictionary of Sacramental Worship*, ed. Peter E. Fink SJ (Dublin: Gill and Macmillan, 1990), 1055.

TARIFF PENANCE

Canonical Penance was replaced by different practices. One was deathbed reconciliation. This took place without prior penance and gradually became associated with anointing—Extreme Unction. Another emerging practice was Tariff Penance. This was introduced by Irish missionary monks to Europe. It involved private confession and specific penance. The penance appropriate for each sin was listed in penitential books. This concluded with private reconciliation. This allowed for forgiveness of sins more than once. Due to the tariff, it required a detailed confession so that the confessor could assign the determined penance. Practically, this became a very private procedure. As the role of the confessor developed at this time, the visible role of the community decreased. Sin was seen as a "contaminating stain which put the sinner in debt to God."[3] Reconciliation, then, was viewed not so much with the church community as repaying a debt to God.

Around this time there also developed devotional confession to a chosen confessor, joined with spiritual counsel, as a regular practice for growth in virtue and the eradication of sin. It was a form of spiritual direction.

THE FOURTH LATERAN COUNCIL

At the Fourth Lateran Council in 1215, to overcome a laxity in the reception of Communion, legislation was

3. Ibid.

introduced that required Confession and Communion at Easter as an annual observance. The Confession was to be made to the parish priest and Communion was to be received in the parish church. After this Council the Religious Orders contributed to more frequent confession, without connection to Easter, through their preaching of penance and conversion.

Throughout this period, and since, there has been theological debate concerning how sins were forgiven. The discussion, of its nature, was very technical. While the role of the confessor continually developed, that of the visible community virtually disappeared. The sacrament seemed almost to become a private endeavor focused on one's sins.[4]

THE NEW RITE OF PENANCE

Up until 1973, when the *Rite of Penance* was published, this remained the case. The 1973 rite tried to regain a communal sense of the sacrament as well as the concept that the sacrament is concerned with one's future life of conversion as much as one's past life of sin.

It is evident from this brief outline of the history of the sacrament that the Church is continually growing into the true meaning of penance and reconciliation. She has expressed it in different ways through the centuries, often as a response to particular situations.

4. See Council of Trent, Session XIV, *De sacramento Paenitentiae*.

Today the Church has arrived at a critical moment in the history of the sacrament. We have emerged from a period of apparent certainty when the focus of the sacrament was sin and hell to a time when a new focus is emerging. This in-between moment can be a time of great uncertainty. However, what remains consistent throughout the history of the sacrament is the power of God to forgive and our need to be forgiven. Pope Benedict XVI emphasized this when he wrote in his *Pastoral Letter to the Catholics of Ireland*:

> I encourage you to discover anew the sacrament of Reconciliation and to avail yourselves more frequently of the transforming power of its grace.[5]

Obviously Pope Benedict XVI believes that the sacrament of Reconciliation has a powerful role to play in the future of the Church. This power comes from what he describes as the grace of the sacrament. It is necessary to discover what that grace is and how it manifests itself. The source of the grace and indeed the manifestation of the grace can be described by the word reconciliation. Reconciliation captures the heart of the sacrament because reconciliation implies a restoration of positive relationship. In considering the sacrament of Reconciliation, we are looking at a particular expression of a relationship between two people: Jesus and me. The

---

5. Pope Benedict XVI, *Pastoral Letter of the Holy Father Pope Benedict XVI to the Catholics of Ireland* (Dublin: Veritas, 2010), 17.

sacrament of Reconciliation expresses something of the relationship that Jesus has with me. The sacrament situates this relationship in the context of the Church— the Body of Christ. We live our relationship with Jesus in his body.

THE GIFT OF FREEDOM

WHEN WE THINK ABOUT THE SACRAMENT OF Reconciliation our thoughts most often focus on ourselves and our sinfulness. The role of God in some sense might even appear secondary. However, the sacrament of Reconciliation is primarily that sacred place and moment when God confesses. The primary confessor in the sacrament is God. What does God confess? God confesses his love, his forgiveness, his gratitude, his confidence, his trust and his belief in us. It is God's confession that enables us to confess. God's attitude creates a safe and non-judgmental environment for us to be true to ourselves and to be true to the one who loves us most.

Our understanding of the sacrament reveals our image of God. If our image of God is one of an uncompromising judge, then the sacrament can fill us with dread. This is the God of the Big Book who writes down all our sins and forgets none of them. And when we die, God consults the Big Book to see if we have done enough to gain heaven or not! When we think of God in this uncompromising way we can believe that it is part of God's role in the ongoing story of creation to keep hell open by sending people to it! In fact we can believe that God takes pleasure in sending people to hell just to show them who is boss. When hell is mentioned today a whole new discussion emerges. There are those who believe hell exists and those who don't. There are those who seem to take great pride in telling us that hell is probably full and there are those who say that the very presence of hell must be a denial of God's boundless forgiveness. *The Catechism of the Catholic Church*, when discussing hell, does so in the context of our relationship with God, with one another, and with ourselves. It very clearly describes this relationship as a relationship of love.

> We cannot be united with God unless we freely choose to love him. But we cannot love God if we sin gravely against him, against our neighbor or against ourselves.[6]

The consequence of positively and freely choosing not to love God means being separated from God. This is hell. The *Catechism* states:

> This state of definitive self-exclusion from communion with God and the blessed is called "hell."
> (CCC, *1033*)

The existence of hell respects the gift of free will that God gives to each one of us. If hell did not exist then we would have no choice but to be in relationship with God. We could not choose to be otherwise. God would be prohibiting our choices. God allowed hell to

---

6. *Catechism of the Catholic Church* (Dublin: Veritas, 1994), 1033. (Henceforth *CCC*.)

exist because to do otherwise would have been forcing himself into the lives of those who do not want him in their lives. Therefore, the existence of hell enables us to take responsibility for our lives and to make choices in our lives. The presence of hell allows God to respect the decisions we make in our lives even if those decisions bring tremendous pain to God. The existence of free choice does not mean that God does not care. Rather, God is the parent who desires that his children freely make positive, life-giving decisions in their lives. However, God does not force those decisions. He trusts. When, or if, that trust is betrayed he trusts again and again and again. God never stops trusting. God then, rather than being portrayed as an uncompromising judge, might be more accurately understood as the loving parent who never gives up on his/her child.

This image of God as the parent who continually trusts and respects seems to be at odds with the image of God as the uncompromising judge. The uncompromising judge is not the person that Jesus revealed. In John's gospel Jesus says:

> For God sent his Son into the world not to condemn the world, but so that through him the world might be saved. No one who believes in him will be condemned; but whoever refuses to believe is condemned already, because he refused to believe in the name of God's only Son. On these grounds is sentence pronounced: that though the light has

come in to the world men have shown they prefer darkness to the light because their deeds were evil.
(John 3:17–19)

God does not judge. God does not need to judge. We judge ourselves. Ronald Rolheiser says:

When Jesus speaks of God, he never speaks of God as dealing both life and death, but only as dealing life. Death has its origins elsewhere, as does lying, rationalization, bitterness, hardness of heart, and hell. To say that God does not create hell or send anyone there does not downplay the existence of evil and sin or the danger of eternal punishment; it only pinpoints their origins and makes clear who it is who makes the judgment and who it is who does the sentencing. God does neither; he neither creates hell nor sends anyone to it. We do both.[7]

If God is not the uncompromising judge—the one to be feared—then who is God? Is God the loving parent? In other words, who is God who takes the initiative in the sacrament of Reconciliation?

7. Ronald Rolheiser, "God judges no one," *The Catholic Herald* (25 September 2009).

WHO IS GOD?

Jesus used stories to answer the question "Who is God?" The Prodigal Son is one of these stories (Luke 15:11–32). Do we recognize the father in this story? Sometimes we can overlook the actions of the father and take them for granted as we focus on the two sons. Here is a man who has obviously worked very hard all his life. He has been successful in his work. He seemed to have quite a bit of property and money. We don't hear about the man's wife. Perhaps she has died. Perhaps this man has reared his two sons on his own. We know from the end of the story when he declares to his older son that all he has is his, that his sons were the center of his life and all that he did he did for them. So this is a loving, selfless, caring and competent man. He is a good father.

Imagine the pain this father felt when his younger son asked him for all that he would get when his father died. This son couldn't wait for his father to die. In a sense, his father was taking too long to die and this is what his son told him when he asked for his inheritance. The son wished his father was dead and he let his father know that. This must have been a devastating blow for the father. He must have questioned himself: Where did I go wrong with this boy? What has happened? Yet, instead of arguing or questioning he gave his son exactly what he asked for. This father did not even resort to self-pity. He didn't try emotional blackmail. He didn't ask his son how he could abandon his father in his old age after all that he had done for him. He did not condemn his son. Rather, he simply gave him what he asked for immediately with no strings attached and no threats either. He didn't say, "If you leave here now you will never be welcomed back." He seems to have said nothing. He let his son go. It must have been so difficult.

The son went. He did what he did. When times were good he never thought about going home. Then times got bad. He had nothing. In his poverty, he realized that he still had something. He had his father. This was a great testament to his father, that the son knew that he could go back home after all that he had done. Yet he didn't trust his father nearly as much as his father trusted him. This is obvious because the son did what so many do when they have got it wrong and have to face up to it. The son spent the whole journey home thinking about the story he was going to tell his father. It is such a natural thing to do. We think: *I will say this and then I will say that*. We try to get our story as convincing as possible. We try to work out our bargaining position. We even try to work out our defenses. It is a very natural reaction.

While all of this was going on and indeed from the moment his son left, the father did only one thing: wait. The very fact that he waited reveals that he never gave up hope in his son. He continued to believe in his son, even after all he had done. He simply waited. This act of waiting reveals the tremendous humility of this father.

Then the waiting was over. The father saw his son coming home, destitute. He immediately felt compassion for his son. He experienced his son's pain. His love for his son drove him to share this pain. He ran to his son. This old man ran out to his son and he hugged him. He held him. This was a moment of complete tenderness and acceptance. When asked what human maturity is, Patrick Mathias, a former psychiatrist with the L'Arche Community responded, "tenderness."[8] This father was a mature man. His waiting for his younger son was over. This was a moment of utter joy. It didn't matter to the father how his son looked or what he had done. All that mattered to him was that his son had come home. In the embrace the father humbly communicated his love, his acceptance, his trust and his belief in his son. The son was overwhelmed. He wanted to explain. He wanted to open negotiations. The father wouldn't let him. He just wanted to celebrate. He wanted to have a party. He wanted to tell everybody that his son had come home. That is just what he did. He had the fatted calf killed and they celebrated.

We know that his older son was not impressed. He was offended by his father's actions. He probably thought that his father was a fool. Yet the father treated him

8. Jean Vanier, "Letter of Jean Vanier" (Spring, 2011).

with the same love and respect with which he treated his younger son. When he heard that his older son would not come in the father left the celebration and went out to him. He listened to him. He understood him. Then, in a moment of deep tenderness and love, he revealed to his older son that they were one—that they shared completely in each other's lives. There was no distance between them. They were united. Their unity was so strong it could be open to including this son and brother who had left but now had come back home. This reveals the utter confidence that the father had in the relationship that he had with his older son.

This is an incredible father. This story is the representation of the Father who invites us to celebrate the sacrament of Reconciliation. This is the Father who takes the initiative in the sacrament of Reconciliation. It is into the loving embrace of this Father that we enter when we celebrate the sacrament. Therefore, the sacrament is a moment of deep tenderness and love between a parent and a child.

Maybe we struggle with this image of God just as much as we struggle with the image of God as the uncompromising judge. Maybe it is difficult to claim the profound reality that we are children of God. We like to grow up. We like to be adults. To be children is to be weak and dependent. To be adults is to be strong and independent. Perhaps too often we are taught that to be successful we need to be self-sufficient. It is a sign of weakness to have

to rely on another. These concepts can affect our relationships. They can actually make it difficult to relate
because we are always trying to prove something—to
prove that we are adults and capable of living life on our
own. Yet the invitation of Jesus is to become like little
children. He tells us:

> In truth I tell you, unless you change and become
> like little children you will never enter the kingdom
> of Heaven.
>
> *(Mt. 18:3)*

It is hard to become like a little child. It is hard to
become aware of our dependence on our parents. This is
something that we feel we have to grow out of not grow
into. Little children are vulnerable and fragile. Often we
want to leave those feelings behind. They are feelings
that bring us insecurity. Yet in each one of us we know
that there is a child. We know that there is vulnerability.
We know that there is fragility. We know that there
is a need for a parent—for love—for unconditional
acceptance. Fr. Peter McVerry, a Jesuit priest who works
with people who are homeless, says that every person
who is homeless that he has met is looking primarily
not for a home, but to be loved—to be accepted. It can
be so hard to admit this need to be loved and accepted
because admitting it seems to go against the powerful
thrust to adulthood and self-sufficiency. Yet, to truly
experience the gift of the sacrament of Reconciliation

we need to listen and respond to the part of us that never grows old—the little child. Like the prodigal we need to be able to kneel, broken, before the Father, and allow his love and forgiveness to seep into us. In a sense that is the sacrament of Reconciliation. It is the empowering, accepting embrace of God. It is in this embrace that God confesses. The amazing thing about God's confession is that it reveals that God believes in us far more than we will ever believe in God. God believes in us far more than we will ever believe in ourselves. This is the incredible reality of the sacrament and a reality that can often be lost because we are so focused on ourselves that we don't think about God or his feelings.

God has utter confidence in all of his creation. Each one of us is part of that creation. God has utter confidence in each one of us. This confidence is expressed in the sacrament of Confirmation. In that sacrament God trusts us with his life. This trust that God has in us is so dramatically portrayed in the story of the calming of the storm (Mk. 4:35–41). In this story Jesus gets into the boat prepared for sleep. He has a cushion with him for his head! Two things that are required for a good sleep are security and contentment. It is not easy to sleep when you don't feel secure. It is not easy to sleep when you are worried and lack contentment. Jesus slept well on the boat. Despite the great gale and the waves breaking into the boat, Jesus slept. This is evidence of the trust and the confidence that he had in his friends who were steering the boat. The problem, of course, was that the Apostles did not have confidence in themselves. They doubted the trust that Jesus had in them. They panicked and woke the sleeping, trusting Jesus. Jesus struggled to understand why they did not have the faith that he had in them. They had faith in Jesus because they woke him to help them but they lacked faith in themselves.

Knowing us completely, God has utter trust in us. Therefore we don't need to prove ourselves to God. We are just called to trust in his confidence. It is this confidence that is so powerfully expressed in the sacrament of Reconciliation. It is the confidence that enabled the father to wait and wait for his son to return. It was the confidence that enabled the father to go out to his older son and declare that they were one—no competition between them—neither having anything to prove to the other. It was trust in this confidence that enabled the prodigal to fall on his knees in a childlike embrace with his father. It was insecurity in the face of this confidence that prohibited the older son from entering into an embrace with his father.

The confidence of the Father comes from his deep humility—a fruit of his profound love. This humility enabled him simply to wait on his young son to come home. Our experience of the sacrament of Reconciliation can be truly transformed when we focus on the humility of God. St. Teresa of Avila, in describing prayer, said:

In prayer God simply looks at me lovingly and humbly.

This humility of God is expressed so beautifully in another appropriate image of our relationship with God, celebrated in the sacrament of Reconciliation. Yes, God is the patient, loving, humble father, waiting for us to come home but God is also the spouse whose love is forgiving and unshakable. We are called to be in a faithful relationship with God. At the heart of this faithful relationship is humility. It is God's humble heart that enables God to be in this faithful relationship with us. In the book of the prophet Isaiah we read:

Like a young man marrying a virgin, so will the one
    who built you wed you,
and as the bridegroom rejoices in his bride, so will
    your God rejoice in you.
(Isa. 62:5)

Here we experience the young, pure and innocent love of a newly married couple that enables God to rejoice in the one to whom God is committed. This too is the heart of friendship, where one reveals what is most beautiful in the other and rejoices in that beauty.

However, even though our God is faithful to us, we have often failed to remain faithful to him. This has been the story of humanity from the beginning. We have been unfaithful to God. When that happens we damage our relationship with God. How does God react to this unfaithfulness? Does God abandon us? Does God separate from us?

The answer to these questions is no. Again in the book of the prophet Isaiah God says:

> my love for you will never leave you
> and my covenant of peace with you will never be
> shaken. *(Isa. 54:10)*

In the book of the prophet Hosea God's awareness of our unfaithfulness is so obvious yet God does not abandon us. Our unfaithfulness wounds God but God does not give up on us. God's desire is to lure us into the wilderness and speak to our hearts (Hosea 2:16). When God speaks to our hearts, God is confident that we will respond as we did when we were young, when we were full of enthusiastic love. Perhaps the sacrament of Reconciliation is that moment when our lover God lures us into the wilderness of our lives and speaks to our hearts. In that moment the humble heart of God speaks to our own broken heart. The conversation is so sacred that our awareness is transformed from our own brokenness to the love that emits from the heart of God.

The sacrament of Reconciliation, then, is an intense moment of prayer—an intense moment of awareness that God is looking at me lovingly and humbly. This is an incredible reality about our God. It is a reality that is beautifully expressed in the book of the prophet Isaiah:

Thus says the Lord: With heaven my throne
and earth my footstool,
what house could you build for me, what place could
you make for my rest? All of this was made by my
hand and all of this is mine—it is the Lord who
speaks. But my eyes are drawn to the person
of humble and contrite spirit who trembles at my word.
 (Isa. 66:1–2)

Our God has the power to do whatever God wills and yet with this power God chooses to be in relationship with us. God has no need to be dependent on us but he desires that we enter into relationship with him. God is drawn to us. God is attracted to us. God desires us and is willing to wait humbly on us, no matter how long that wait will be. One simple and beautiful way of celebrating the end of God's wait is when we celebrate the sacrament of Reconciliation.

WHO AM I?

My eyes are drawn.
  (Isa. 66:1–2)

These are the words of God from the book of the prophet Isaiah. How could any human being possibly attract the attention of God? Perhaps many human beings would not want to attract the attention of God because they believe that he would only find flaws in them. So often we can have a very poor self-image. We can feel inadequate and unworthy in the sight of God. The image we have of ourselves is vitally important when we are thinking about our relationship with God and when we are thinking about our celebration of the sacrament of Reconciliation. How do we perceive ourselves? Do we have a positive or a negative self-image? Often, in preparation for the sacrament of Reconciliation our self-image can plummet. We are focusing so much on how bad we are! We are almost apologizing if we don't have some big sin to confess! We seem to believe that in order to get the full benefit of the sacrament, we need to be really big sinners. However, if we think we are really big sinners we may be too uncomfortable to celebrate the sacrament. It all gets very complicated! Maybe we struggle to understand what being a sinner really is. Richard Rohr, when discussing sinners, says:

The word signifies not moral inferiors so much
as people who do not know *who* they are and *whose*
they are, people who have no connection to their
inherent dignity and importance. They have to struggle for it by all kinds of futile performances.[9]

So who are we? And whose are we? These seem to
be the questions that need to be answered. Answering
these questions can be difficult because they require that
we stop and face the truth about ourselves. Often this
can appear to be very threatening. Personal reflection can
be extremely challenging. It reminds me of a story that
my father told me about a man who was cycling. He was
not very confident on his bicycle. One day as he was
coming down a hill at quite a fast speed he noticed
someone walking towards him. As he approached the
person walking he shouted, 'Don't speak to me or I'll
fall off!' Perhaps this is an image of how many of us
live our lives. We live at great speed with very little
confidence in our ability. Maybe we are afraid to stop
in the midst of the rat race of life. It can seem safer,
somehow, to keep going trying not to think too much
in case it would be just that—too much. If we live
like this we won't be able to create the time and the
space we need to try to answer the questions: Who
are we? Whose are we? The result of this seems to
be what Rohr describes as a struggle with all sorts of

9. Richard Rohr, *The Naked Now* (New York: Crossroads Publishing
   Company, 2009), 21.

futile performances. These performances can bring us to places that we would never have chosen to go and leave us in situations in which we would never have chosen to be. Most of our disasters in life are a result of our lack of reflection and our lack of awareness of who we are and indeed whose we are.

So, who are we? Whose are we? To answer these questions, I think we need to go to the Good News again and to one particular book in the Old Testament— The Song of Songs. This love poem reveals who we are and whose we are. This love poem contains a lot more youthful energy than the story of the prodigal father. In a sense the story of the prodigal father is a homecoming story. The Song of Songs is a setting-out poem. However, the way we set out may well have a lot of bearing on how we will come home. So the two stories are very necessary.

God loves each and every one of us. This is a statement that we have heard so often and of which we probably have some awareness. The Song of Songs reveals the dynamic, energetic way that God loves us. God is in love with us. God pursues us, but will always wait for our response. In the Song of Songs God reveals to each one of us how beautiful we are. He says:

> How beautiful you are, my love,
> how beautiful you are!
>   *(S. of S. 1:16)*

Who are we? We are the beautiful creation of God that God desires. Nothing or nobody can ever take that reality away from us. We are beautiful and God is in love with us. But our God is a shy pursuer. Yes, God comes leaping over the mountains and bounding over the hills like a young gazelle but then God stops. God waits behind the wall. God looks in the window and then God calls. God invites. Our God says:

> Come then, my love, my lovely one, come.
> My dove, hiding in the clefts of the rock,
> in the coverts of the cliff,
> show me your face, let me
> hear your voice; for your
> voice is sweet
> and your face is beautiful.
>   *(S. of S. 2:13–14)*

This is how much our God loves us. This love is enduring. Nothing can bring God's love for us to an end.

> Love no flood can quench,
> no torrents drown.
>   *(S. of S. 8:7)*

When we respond to this lively and life-giving love that God has for us we maintain the joy of our youth. We receive energy and life. We are able to say with the bride in the Song of Songs:

Draw me in your footsteps. Let us run.
  (S. of S. 1:4)

We can run in the footsteps of our God when we are confident in God's love for us and our own beauty. We can run in the footsteps of our God when we know who we are—God's beloved—and when we know whose we are—God's. The much quoted line from St. Augustine is so true:

Our hearts are restless until they rest in God.

When we rest in God we can have a childlike peace. That childlike peace gives us confidence in ourselves and the energy we need to live life to the full.

We are called to celebrate the sacrament of Reconciliation conscious and aware of our original goodness; aware that we are fundamentally good; that we are beautiful—now. Sometimes the 'now' can make the whole process much more difficult. We might be able to believe that we were good once—maybe when we were little children. We might be able to think that we could be beautiful again if we changed this and fixed that. To accept that we are fundamentally good and beautiful as we are today is probably too much to ask many of us to do. In many ways this is very understandable in the society and world that we live in.

We live in a society that has a very restricted and superficial understanding of what is good and beautiful. It has all to do with appearance and shape. Someone somewhere has decreed that thin is beautiful and that success and fame are good. Many of us buy into these ridiculous definitions. One proof of this is the number of people who are having cosmetic surgery today. God has made each of us unique and beautiful but our confidence in God's creation is being continually undermined. Sadly, too often we don't have the confidence to trust in what God has made.

Bill Cullen, an Irish businessman, tells a story about his granny in his book, *Golden Apples.*[10] He tells that even though they were very poor his granny made him do one thing every day when he got up. She trained him to stand in front of the mirror and look at himself looking out and say: 'You are terrific!' It seems to be a very simple thing to do but try it and try to mean it! Cullen believed that his granny gave him the confidence he needed to become a very successful businessman. Do many of us really believe that we are terrific? What does it mean to be terrific? Does it mean to be perfect and able to do anything? Does it mean to have no weakness? I don't think so. Are we not terrific when we accept that we are originally good and also that we have original sin? Our beauty comes from the whole truth about ourselves. That whole truth involves all that is good in us and all that is broken in us. We are a mixture of both. However, the power of our brokenness decreases when we realize that we are the beloved of God. The brokenness remains but

10. Bill Cullen, *Golden Apples* (London: Hodder and Stoughton Ltd, 2005).

when our anguish decreases—an anguish that comes from believing that we are not lovable—our compulsion to give in to our sin becomes less and less intense. Then our awareness of our beauty increases and gives us confidence. All of this happens through the power of God's love. When we accept this, our self-image is transformed and we are able to reflect more honestly about our lives and celebrate the sacrament of Reconciliation.

Our starting point for all reflection and celebration needs to be that we are fundamentally beautiful, aware of all that our beauty entails. That seems to be the only true place to start. If we start somewhere else our foundation is possibly not true and that makes our journey much more difficult. To start at this point of our truth and beauty, our original goodness, is to start at the core of our being. It is to start on the original sacred foundation of who we are. It is to start in that part of us that can never be damaged or contaminated. It is that place where we are alone with God. It is the place of conscience. *Gaudium et Spes* states that:

> Conscience is the most secret core and sanctuary of a man. There he is alone with God, whose voice echoes in his depths.[11]

Our conscience then is where we are at one with God. It is that place within us where the mind of God is our mind and where the ways of God are our ways. Etty

11. Second Vatican Council, *Gaudium et Spes* (Dublin: Dominican, 1977), no. 16.

Hillesum, who perished at Auschwitz, was describing perhaps the place of conscience when she said:

> I regained contact with myself, with the deepest and best in me, which I call God.[12]

Conscience, then, is that place where there is complete unity and peace between us and God. It is Eden, the place of Adam and Eve before they ate the forbidden fruit. Our conscience, then, predates the fall. That place of conscience exists in each one of us. Since it exists God can trust us enough to enable Jesus to sleep on the boat. God trusts us because fundamentally in that privileged place of conscience we are at one with him. Our conscience is that place within which Walter Macken speaks about:

> The inside of you is like a well, a deep well about which you know very little. That must be your soul, where all the real things take place. And if it is a right deep place, and has been tended by your head, then he supposed that God would be deep down in there whispering to you always about the realities, so that would be the real fair land, deep down in yourself.[13]

When we connect to the core of our being—to the real fair land within us; to that place of truth and beauty, that place of original goodness; to, in the words of Rohr, our inherent dignity and importance—we are united with God. There is

---

12. Patrick Woodhouse, *Etty Hillesum: A Life Transformed* (London: Continuum, 2009), 39.
13. Walter Macken, *Seek the Fair Land* (London: Pan Books, 1962), 299.

no distance between us. We share fully in his life. That is why Blessed John Henry Newman could say:

> Certainly, if I am obliged to bring religion into after-dinner toasts, (which indeed does not seem quite the thing) I shall drink—to the Pope, if you please—still, to Conscience first, and to the Pope afterwards.[14]

Newman was clearly stating that nothing comes between us and God—not even the Pope. The Church teaches this very clearly too when it states:

> Man has the right to act in conscience and in freedom so as personally to make moral decisions. "He must not be forced to act contrary to his conscience. Nor must he be prevented from acting according to his conscience, especially in religious matters."
>
> (CCC, *1782*)

It is in the context of our conscience—our sacred unity with God—that we are called to make every decision in our lives. We make our decisions in the depths of our being, where God's voice echoes. In the depths of our being, in the real fair land, in that sanctuary there is uncontaminated truth and beauty. Therefore, at the core of our being we are good and we know what is right and good. This knowing what is right is much more than simply what might feel right at a particular time. It is

---

14. John Henry Newman, *Letter to the Duke of Norfolk* (1875), Section 5.

truth. It is objective. Even though it is objective it is not static or complete. It cannot be static or complete because fundamentally it is a relationship—our relationship with God. As Walter Macken suggests, we may know very little about it. However, our relationship with God has the potential to grow and develop as we grow and develop. Therefore, our conscience can grow and develop. It needs to grow and develop. Perhaps we could describe this growth and development in the words of T.S. Eliot:

> We shall not cease from exploration, and the end
> of all our exploring will be to arrive where we started
> and know the place for the first time.
>
> *(T.S. Eliot, "Little Giddings,"* Four Quartets)

As we develop our conscience we are exploring how God wants us to relate to the world at any given time. This exploration will lead us back to that sacred sanctuary within us where we know what it means to be united with God. In that place of unity with God we know justice from injustice. We know love from hate. We know truth from lies. In that sanctuary we know right from wrong. It is part of us from the beginning. I realized this through the actions of my nephew Eoghan when he was aged two. He seemed to instinctively know what was right and wrong. He would say sorry to his mother before he hit his older sister!

This brings us to another issue with conscience. Eoghan knew that it was wrong to hit his sister yet he still did it.

Why? Why do we choose to go against our conscience? This is again freedom and emphasizes the massive risk God takes when he trusts us. We could understand Eoghan going against his conscience because he was only two and unaware that he had a conscience. It is his parents, his god-parents, and the Christian community's responsibility to help him as he gets older to realize that he has a conscience and to develop that conscience. But what about the adult—the one who is aware of their conscience—how or why do they choose to do what is wrong? Yes, they have the freedom to choose what is wrong but why do they? *Gaudium et Spes* tells us that when we are faithful to our conscience we

> [Christians] are joined with the rest of men in the search for truth, and for the genuine solutions to the numerous problems which arise in the life of individuals from social relationships.
>
> *(Gaudium et Spes no. 16)*

When we are faithful to our conscience we live moral lives in right relationships with God, others, and with the world. In other words, when we are in unity with God we are at peace with our sisters and brothers and indeed with all God's creation. However, this often does not happen. Often we make decisions that are contrary to our unity with God. How do we make these decisions? One of the ways is through ignorance, by not developing our conscience through no fault of our own. The other way is when we are not motivated by truth and beauty. If that becomes a habit we lose contact with our conscience—with our inner sanctuary—with God. This is what happened to Adam and Eve. However, even though God's people lost contact with their conscience—with God—God never lost contact with them. He gave them his law. He gave them his prophets. Ultimately he gave them his Son, his Spirit and his Church. All these gifts from God are given to lead us back to the sanctuary within us and to know the place for the first time. All these gifts are given to help us to live and act in unity with God. It is when we come to know the law and the prophets of the Old Testament better, when we come to know Jesus better and are more and more aware of God's Spirit in us, when we come to live in the Church more fully, when we understand the teaching of the Church, rooted in the gospel, that we get a deeper knowledge of the core of our being, where God lives, and we inform and develop our conscience. This is so necessary if we are to accept God's gift of reconciliation.

The place of conscience, however, can be a very lonely place. At times our fear of loneliness can lead us to follow something other than our conscience. It can be lonely to be in sacred unity with God. When everyone around you seems to be doing something different than you it can be hard to be present in the sanctuary that is your conscience. However, it is real love that drives us to that sanctuary and it is real love that gives us the courage to form our actions from that sanctuary. This is clearly revealed in the story of the Good Samaritan (Lk. 10:29–37). The priest and the Levite were unable to stop and help the one who was wounded. Perhaps their inability came from a fear. Maybe the source of that fear was the fact that they wanted the group they belonged to to think well of them. I have no doubt but that they noticed the man who was wounded. Deep within them, in that place of conscience, they wanted to help him but they were unfree. Their ability to love was restricted and inhibited because they lacked courage. That lack of courage may have come from their lack of identity as beloved children of God. Perhaps they got their identity from being a priest or a Levite before being a beloved child of God. When that happens the way to the sanctuary of conscience is obstructed. It was the Samaritan who was driven by real love. He had the confidence not to obstruct that love. He did what was not expected of him. He did this not out of duty but out of love. That is so obvious in the fact that he promised to come back and take responsibility for the wounded man's care. The Samaritan man must have known love and so was free to love.

When we start the journey to reconciliation and forgiveness then, we start with two basic truths. The first is that God loves us humbly. The second is that we are lovable because we are fundamentally true, good and beautiful, created in the image and likeness of God. It is in this context that we are called to prepare to celebrate the sacrament of Reconciliation. It is this context of love that inspires repentance and sorrow as well as conversion and new life.

In the sacrament of Reconciliation God humbly confesses his love for us and we humbly confess our need for that love and the confidence that it brings. We confess our desire to be at home in the sanctuary of our lives—in that place of pure love. When we are aware of God's love we cannot help but share that love. God's love is so powerful and immense that we cannot keep it to ourselves. Our awareness of God's love will naturally transform our lives. It will naturally affect all our relationships. That is why our experience of God's love comes primarily through God's family—our community. It is expressed in our relationships with one another. This is why we celebrate the sacrament of Reconciliation in the community. In the sacrament God confesses his love in the context of forgiveness—the fruit of love.

FORGIVENESS

WHAT IS FORGIVENESS? WHEN WE SPEAK ABOUT forgiveness what do we really mean? It is a frequently used word. We even have sayings like, 'Forgive and forget.' But what is it all about?

Sometimes forgiveness can be perceived as weakness. It can be seen as giving in—allowing the person who hurt you to get away with what they did. This then can be seen as something very negative. When we are unable to forgive we can at times become bitter. When this happens, when we become bitter, forgiveness seems almost unobtainable. When we are bitter we are unfree. Our bitterness drains us of our positive energy. It leads to self-destruction. Bitterness leads us to live life with clenched fists rather than with open hands. Bitterness leads us to blame. We blame others for the hurt, and maybe rightly so, but in bitterness the blame can then extend beyond that and we can become obsessed with blaming and with the person who has hurt us.

Often it can seem so much easier to blame than to forgive. At so many levels in our society we spend more time and energy trying to find someone to blame than we do in trying to forgive. Blaming makes us right! It gives us all the excuses we need to retaliate or to condemn. Blaming allows us the permission to treat others in a less than Christian way in the name of justice. Blaming has our world, our society, many of our families and indeed often our own hearts paralyzed. Think of the wars that are raging in our world. Often the defense for going into war is that they attacked us first and they need to be controlled and taught a lesson. In our own society, riots and violence are often blamed on somebody else. Again they are used to show who is in control and to try to settle old scores. Even in our families we can refuse to speak to others because we have been wronged. We can cause such division and anger in our families because we are preoccupied with blaming someone else for an action that has hurt us.

When we enter into the blame game and the blame can be attributed to somebody tens or even hundreds of years ago it allows us to arm ourselves to the teeth with self-righteousness and with the means for violence and destruction. We can then convince ourselves and others that we are fighting for what is right—for freedom and justice.

But Peter says to Jesus, "How often must I forgive?" (Mt. 18:21). Jesus says, "As often as you are hurt." In other words, every time. What Jesus says is not new. In the book of Ecclesiasticus we are told that resentment and anger are foul things. Vengeance only results in vengeance.

> Forgive your neighbor the hurt he does you, and
> when you pray, your sins will be forgiven. If a man

nurses anger against another,

can he then demand compassion from the Lord?

   (Sir. 28:2–3)

But it is not easy to forgive where hurt exists and blame is being attributed. Forgiveness does not sit easily here. You see it can be so hard to forgive. It can be so hard even to use the language of forgiveness. When we are hurt and we blame, we have a clear role and there are obvious things that we do. We retaliate in some way or we become a victim. What do we do if we decide to forgive? How do we live out that decision?

After September 11th, President George Bush said that the American nation would not be defeated—that they would find the terrorists and deal with them. He declared a war on terrorism. Just imagine if he had said on behalf of the American nation, "I forgive the terrorists." What would have happened? Imagine if he had declared a war on want, a war on division, a war on revenge. When we forgive, we respect, we listen, and we let the other, the one who has hurt us, go and so we free ourselves. It is so, so difficult. It is not a moment in time but it is a long, long process. Forgiveness is a process that involves daily decisions. Even though it has been spoken about since Old Testament times, it is still a very new language and a hard language to learn. It is not the language that many of us use because it is a radical language that goes beyond justice—goes beyond an eye for an eye. It is a language that arms itself only in humility and respect for oneself and the other.

Forgiveness is when you don't hit back or become a victim. It is when you have the freedom as a beloved child of God to love the other person, to free them from the anger or violence that is paralyzing them, to see them as a wound to be healed rather than an enemy to be defeated. Blame and retaliation only paralyze both persons.

But forgiveness can be so difficult. Yet, each time we pray the Our Father we pray:

Forgive us our sins as we forgive those who sin against us.

Jean Vanier says that the whole gospel of Jesus is contained in these words. He goes on to say:

Forgiveness is not, however, just a one-time event where we go up to the person who has hurt us and give them a big hug. Forgiveness is a process. To move from hate to acceptance and love is a long journey. Even when we have been deeply hurt, we can grow into forgiveness.[15]

Jean Vanier then outlines three movements in forgiveness. The first two of these movements he presents in the context of profound and real examples:

15. Jean Vanier, *Drawn into the Mystery of Jesus through the Gospel of John* (London: Darton, Longman and Todd, 2004), 152.

Some years ago I spoke with a woman in Rwanda. Seventy-five members of her family had been killed. "I have so much hate in my heart," she said, "and everyone is talking about reconciliation!" I asked her if she wanted to kill those people who had killed her family. "No," she answered. "Too many people have been killed already!" I said to her: "Do you know that the first movement in the process of forgiveness is not to seek revenge? You are on the road to forgiveness."

I heard about a woman who had been put in prison because of a man's false testimony. She did not know about Jesus but met regularly for support with a religious sister. One day she met Jesus and discovered the gospel message. It was a revelation for her. The Sister asked her if she could look at forgiving the man who had given the false testimony. "No," she replied. "He has hurt me too much." "But," she added, "I pray for him each day, that he may be liberated from all the evil in him." The second step in the process of forgiveness is to pray for those who consciously or unconsciously have hurt us.

Another step is to become conscious of who the person is who has hurt us, how he or she came to be as they are. Where are the fears in them? How did these fears come about? They, too, have been deeply hurt somewhere. Little by little, we begin to understand them.[16]

16. Ibid., 152–153.

When we enter into the movement of forgiveness we begin to recognize in the one to be forgiven, not an enemy to be defeated but someone who has a wound to be healed. This is a different and much gentler way of engaging with others.

Immaculee Ilibagiza is from Rwanda. During the genocide of 1994 her family was brutally murdered. For ninety-one days, she and seven other women were confined to a small bathroom in a pastor's house. They were not able to make noise as they were being hunted by hundreds of people with machetes wanting to kill them. In this horrendous situation Immaculee discovered forgiveness:

One night I heard screaming not far from the house, and then a baby crying. The killers must have slain the mother and left her infant to die in the road. The child wailed all night; by morning, its cries were feeble and sporadic, and by nightfall, it was silent. I heard dogs snarling nearby and shivered as I thought about how that baby's life had ended. I prayed for God to receive the child's innocent soul, and then asked him, "How can I forgive people who would do such a thing to an infant?"

I heard his answer as clearly as if we'd been sitting in the same room chatting: "You are all my children ... and the baby is with me now."

It was such a simple sentence, but it was the answer to the prayers I'd been lost in for days.

The killers were like children. Yes, they were barbaric creatures who would have to be punished severely for their actions, but they were still children. They were cruel, vicious, and dangerous, as kids sometimes can be, but nevertheless, they were children … Their minds had been infected with the evil that had spread across the country, but their *souls* weren't evil. Despite their atrocities, they were children of God, and I could forgive a child, although it would not be easy … especially when that child was trying to kill me.

In God's eyes, the killers were part of his family, deserving of love and forgiveness … At that moment, I prayed for the killers, for their sins to be forgiven … I took a crucial step towards forgiving the killers that day. My anger was draining from me—I'd opened my heart to God, and he'd touch it with his infinite love. For the first time, I pitied the killers. I asked God to forgive their sins and turn their souls toward his beautiful light.

That night I prayed with a clear conscience and a clean heart. For the first time since I entered the bathroom, I slept in peace.[17]

17. Immaculee Ilibagiza, *Left to Tell* (California: Hay House, 2006), 118–119.

Forgiveness then brings us peace and frees us to love. This is at the heart of the sacrament of Reconciliation. It is a celebration of our freedom to love. Perhaps a lack of forgiveness prohibits us from loving. Maybe when we are closed to receiving forgiveness or closed to forgiving we are paralyzed in our love. We can be hostages to our own lack of forgiveness.

The father in the story of the prodigal son reveals so powerfully how God forgives. When he sees his younger son in the distance making the journey home he runs out to meet him. In the embrace of his son he communicates total and unconditional forgiveness. The father recognizes the wound in his son that only forgiveness can heal. Through his tenderness he heals that wound. However, this is not the only example of forgiveness in the story of the prodigal son. The father also forgives his older son. The moment of forgiveness for the older son comes when the father declares to this son, in the midst of his anger and bitterness:

My son you are with me always and all I have is yours.
 (Lk. 15:31)

The father's forgiveness is revealed in his declaration of profound trust in his older son. This trust and this forgiveness can only come from a place of undiluted love and acceptance. God forgives because he loves. The source of all forgiveness has ultimately to be love. The fruit of forgiveness is also love.

When the woman with the bad name in the town kissed and anointed Jesus' feet he said something remarkable about her. He said:

> I tell you that her sins, her many sins, must have been forgiven her, or she would not have shown such great love.
>
> *(Lk. 7:47)*

Jesus did not deny the reality that this woman was a sinner. He acknowledged the truth of her past life; however, he clearly reveals that it is the forgiveness that she has so obviously received that has enabled her to love. In this woman's case, forgiveness seems to come before an ability to love. Why is it like that? Do we need to know forgiveness before we can truly show love? Perhaps forgiveness and love are different sides of the same coin. Perhaps they are inseparable. What happens when we are forgiven?

I was taught that when I was forgiven by God all my sins were wiped away. I had an image of God with a great big cloth, wiping all the black marks off my soul! In some way it revealed God as a polisher! Is this what happens in forgiveness? If we go back to Richard Rohr's definition of a sinner it might help us to understand forgiveness a bit better. Rohr said that a sinner was a person who did not know who they were or whose they were. If sin is not being connected to the reality of who we are and whose we are, then forgiveness reconnects us to those realities.

The woman with the bad name in the gospel did a very bold thing. She gate-crashed a dinner and proceeded to make a spectacle of herself in the eyes of many. This woman was looked down upon by most people at the dinner. They were embarrassed that she was even in their company. They were horrified that Jesus allowed her to wipe her tears from his feet and to kiss and anoint his feet. The woman knew what the people were thinking about her and saying about her. Most people would not have been able to do what she did. They would not have had the courage or the confidence. So how did she do it? What gave her the courage to do what she did? Jesus gave the answer—love fuelled by forgiveness. That was the source of her courage. In forgiveness this woman rediscovered her fundamental identity that nothing or nobody could take from her. Her fundamental identity revealed to her through forgiveness was that she was good and she was beautiful in the sight of God. It also revealed to her that she was a beloved child of God. With the awareness of that truth she had the freedom to express her love for Jesus in the only way that she could. Forgiveness gave her the freedom to love. The gift of forgiveness, then, is a powerful gift. It reconnects us with the truth of who we are. It is a liberation.

Often, for some strange reason, that can be a painful process. Connecting with the truth of who we are can be a process that we try to avoid. It was something that the older son in the story of the prodigal son struggled to do. It was something that the younger son was forced into doing when he was stripped of everything else. Since we are fundamentally good and beautiful why do we stray from this reality? Surely it is a reality to hold on to constantly. Perhaps it is because we do not believe it. Marianne Williamson believes it is because we are afraid to believe it. She says:

> It is our light, not our darkness that frightens us most. We ask ourselves, Who am I to be brilliant, gorgeous, talented, fabulous? Actually, who are you not to be? You are a child of God. Your playing small does not serve the world. There is nothing enlightened about shrinking so that other people won't feel insecure around you. We are all meant to shine, as children do. We were born to make manifest the glory of God that is within us. It's not just in some of us; it is in everyone. And as we let our own light shine, we unconsciously give other people permission to do the same. As we are liberated from our own fear, our presence automatically liberates others.[18]

Perhaps, then, the sacrament of Reconciliation is a celebration of our liberation. In the sacrament we are liberated from the fear of who we are and so we are free to love and empower others.

---

18. Marianne Williamson, "Our Deepest Fear" in *Return to Love: Reflections on the Principles of A Course in Miracles* (New York: Harper Collins, 1992), 190.

In the sacrament we face the truth. We face the truth that we often struggle to accept and believe. We face the truth that we are fundamentally good and beautiful. We also face the truth of our inability to accept that we are good and beautiful and so we do things that diminish us. We do things that we are not proud of. We do things that we are ashamed of. We let our compulsions and our brokenness dictate our actions. We do things that burden us with guilt. This burden of guilt can paralyze us. It can make us unable to look ourselves or anybody else in the eye and that includes God. We struggle to face ourselves. We struggle to face anybody else. Maybe one of the reasons that people find the sacrament of Reconciliation so difficult is that in it we have to face ourselves, our God and our community in the person of the priest. Facing the reality of our lives and our actions can appear to be more painful than allowing ourselves to get used to feeling guilty.

There is a wonderful and dramatic scene in the film *The Horse Whisperer*. The story is about a young girl from New York who is out riding her horse one day when they are involved in an accident with a lorry. The young girl is badly injured and so is the horse. Both have serious physical and psychological scars from the accident. To help the young girl's recovery her mother realizes that she needs to help the horse's recovery. She is not given much hope that the horse, which has gone quite wild, will be able to recover. In her efforts to find help for the horse she hears about a cowboy in Montana who is described as a horse whisperer. He seems to have a unique bond with animals. She and her daughter travel with the horse to Montana. The horse whisperer starts to work with the horse and it proves to be very difficult. However, the pivotal scene in the film is when the whisperer finally breaks the horse down and makes the horse and the little girl make eye contact with each other. In that moment their bond of trust seems to be re-established. It is a marvelous scene where you can nearly see a guilt being lifted from the horse.

It may seem a strange story to use when speaking about the sacrament of Reconciliation. However, I think that it makes a very important point. In the sacrament we make eye-contact with God and we know that it is okay. Our bond of trust is not so much re-established—since God never loses trust in us; but on our part the bond of trust is rediscovered. In this rediscovery we are released from the burden of guilt. That bond of trust that God has in us, is not in spite of the things we do that cause us guilt, but is in the midst of the full reality of our lives. God does not desire that we try to hide part of our lives from him. Sometimes we can feel that we should only show God the parts of our lives that we consider good—the parts of our lives that we think God would like. God trusts us completely, and is aware of the full story of our lives. That trust is declared again in the sacrament of Reconciliation.

So what do we do with the parts of ourselves that we are ashamed of? What do we do with the parts of ourselves that we want to deny? What do we do with our compulsions and our brokenness? What do we do with the results of those futile performances we engage in as we try to deny who and whose we are? What do we do with our sinfulness?

The city of Munich in Germany might be able to help answer these questions. At the end of the Second World War the city was virtually destroyed. Many of its buildings had been blown up leaving awful destruction and debris in its wake. There was a very great human cost as well. When the war was over the people who were left had to start again. In order to begin their lives again they did a most amazing thing. They gathered all the rubble of the city and brought it to a place on the outskirts of the city where they created a hill—their rubble hill. This rubble of the destruction of their lives was made into a hill. Then in preparation for the 1972 Munich Olympic Games the city of Munich built their Olympic stadium on their rubble hill.

The people of Munich did not try to deny the reality of their history. It was a terrible history. It was a history that contained so much suffering and so much hatred. It was a history that contained shame and humiliation. The obvious thing to do with this type of history would be to hide it. Nobody wants to be reminded constantly of their humiliation, of their shame, of their terrible actions in the past. Yet, by creating the rubble hill the people of Munich did not hide from any of this. By their actions they accepted that the content of the rubble hill was a real and true part of their history that could never be denied. This took such honesty and courage.

It can be so difficult to really admit and accept our history. Maybe our history contains deep hurt to which we have been subjected—hurt that needs to be forgiven if we are to be truly free to live our lives. Our history also contains our sinfulness, our need for reconciliation, our need for forgiveness, our futile performances. It can be hard to admit to what we have done or failed to do without making excuses or comparing ourselves with others. In so many ways in life we never grow up. We struggle to leave the schoolyard mentality behind. You remember when we were caught doing something wrong at school we would invariably find someone else to blame: "It wasn't my fault. He made me do it."

It goes all the way back to Adam and Eve: "It wasn't my fault. She made me do it."

The people of Munich made no such excuses. The rubble of their lives—the rubble of their history—they made into a hill. At that hill they created something beautiful and something positive—their Olympic stadium. They did not allow their past to hold them back; they used it as a platform from which they could enter the future.

Indeed, inside each one of us we have, like the city of Munich, our own rubble hill. That hill is made up of the debris and destruction that was and is part of our lives. It may be the debris of regret, of missed opportunities, of old wounds too bitter to heal. Or maybe it's the destruction of broken relationships, of family pressures, of disappointments, of selfishness, of sinfulness. Often it is the destruction of a lack of forgiveness given or received that makes us unfree. Throughout our lives we accumulate much rubble and this rubble can hold us back and get us down. It can paralyze us and restrict us from being the people we truly are. The rubble that we carry can even cause us to doubt that God really loves us.

Often, unlike the city of Munich, we try to hide the rubble of our lives. We try to put on a good front. We use so much energy denying our rubble. Then the destruction and the debris in our lives can control us. It can make us into people we do not want to be. It can make us into people that we do not like—people who become hard. It can cause us guilt and shame. All that this does is add to the weight of the rubble we carry. We can end up feeling that we are going down a road with no control. It is the road of denial. It is the road of blame. It is the road of no responsibility. It can't be a life giving road

It takes great courage to stop on that road. Yet, in the sacrament of Reconciliation we are invited to stop; just to take a breath; to be honest about our lives; to be honest about it in the safety of God's love; to be truthful about our rubble.

Too often the destruction and debris in our lives, which makes our rubble hill, blind us to the reality of God's love for us and God's belief in us. It is Sr. Wendy Beckett who describes prayer as "standing before God unprotected."[19]

In the prayer that is the sacrament of Reconciliation we are called in a very specific way to stand unprotected before God and to allow our debris and destruction—our rubble—to be seen. The sacrament of Reconciliation is the safest place where we can reveal the debris and destruction of sinfulness in our lives that make up our rubble hill. Through the gift of forgiveness received in the sacrament we are freed from the power of the rubble of our lives. Then, instead of that rubble holding us back and weighing us down, it can become a platform for us to announce the Good News that we are good and beautiful; that God loves us humbly and that God forgives us. It is when we are forgiven and freed from the rubble in our lives that we can make eye contact with ourselves and with our God. Then we know better who we are and whose we are.

19. Sr. Wendy Beckett, *Sister Wendy on Prayer* (London: Continuum, 2006).

SIN

FOR EACH ONE OF US THE CONTENT OF OUR RUBBLE HILL is different, yet one similarity in all our rubble hills is sin, those futile performances, the things we do when we don't know who we are or whose we are. We are all sinners.

If a sinner is one who does not know who or whose he or she is, then sin is an activity carried out whereby we are disconnected from our true self and from God. It is something that diminishes who we are. Our lives are lived out in relationships and we communicate our self-image through how we interact with others. Richard Rohr says:

> Perhaps one reason religion becomes so brittle and legalistic is that it normally tries to define sin as an abstract concept apart from the authentic experience of God.[20]

When Jesus is asked about the commandments he declares that the two greatest commandments are commandments of love. These commandments are not abstract concepts. These are commandments of interaction. They are commandments of relationship. He says:

20. Richard Rohr, *Soul Brothers* (New York: Orbis Books, 2004), 35.

> Listen, Israel, the Lord our God is the one Lord,
> and you must love the Lord your God with all your
> heart, with all your soul, with all your mind and
> with all your strength. You must love your neighbor
> as yourself.
>
> *(Mk. 12:29–30)*

If we keep the commandments of God, we are true to
ourselves and to God. If we are true to ourselves and God
we are people whose lives are marked by love. When we
are untrue to ourselves and to God we sin. Rohr also says:

> If you don't know God, you don't know what sin is.
>
> *(Mk. 12:29–30)*

When sin is situated outside a loving relationship with
God, it can often be seen simply as breaking the law. The
Old Testament focused so much on the law. Necessarily,
the law predominately concerned morality. Sin is easier
to quantify and measure if the focus is just on morality.
An examination of conscience can be reduced to a black
and white check list. However, this approach can dehu-
manize sin. It can detach sin from our relationships and,
in a sense, privatize it. Sin can then be seen as a rejection
of the rules of a club rather than a rejection of a relationship with a person. Then we can live in this bizarre
situation where a relationship with God can be separated
from how a life is lived. In this situation a person may
be familiar with the law but not know who God is. If
Rohr is right, in that case, they cannot know what sin

is either. Knowledge of God is required for knowledge of sin. Therefore, sin is so much more than breaking a law. It is so much more than an abstract concept. Sin is the fracturing of a relationship. It describes the rejection of a trust or a confidence. Sin, then, is when we do not listen and respond positively to the loving call of Jesus. This idea is easy enough to understand in relation to doing right and wrong. However, is the call of Jesus a voluntary call, one we can opt into and out of when it suits us, without responsibility or commitment? To focus the question: did the rich young man commit sin when he felt unable to follow Jesus even though he seemed to be very aware of what was right and wrong and was committed to doing what was right?

This young man seemed to have everything, even a desire to live eternal life, but when Jesus invited him to come with him the young man failed to rise to the challenge of entering into a deeper, fully-committed relationship with Jesus (Lk. 10:17–22). Did the rich young man sin by going away?

Just as there are only two great commandments (loving God and loving our neighbor) the commandments of love, maybe there are only two great sins. If that is the case perhaps the two great sins are the sin of Adam and Eve and the sin of the Innkeeper. All other sins are a manifestation of these two sins.

WHAT WAS THE SIN OF ADAM AND EVE?

They were asked not to eat of the tree of knowledge and they did. They were allowed to do everything except touch this tree and yet they touched it. What motivated them to do that? Why was nearly everything not enough? It reminds me of a sales slogan in a shop in London: When everything is not enough! It is an amazing concept—never being satisfied—always wanting more. Why do we rebel when we are told that there is something that we cannot have or cannot do? Is there a motivation in us to be God in our own lives? This is the sin of Adam and Eve—they wanted to be God. They could not allow God to be God. They wanted to be God themselves. They wanted to have all knowledge themselves because with all knowledge comes power. Maybe this is our fundamental sin. This attempt to be God in our lives is driven by our insecurity when we don't know who or whose we are. We try to prove that we are something we are not because we cannot accept that we are the beautiful, good, and beloved of God. Perhaps we try to prove that we do not need God in our lives, that we are self-sufficient, that we are independent. When this is our attitude we do not have the confidence to love God because we are so desperately trying to prove that we are lovable ourselves. Rather than accepting this reality, in our effort to prove it we can disrespect ourselves and disregard our God. This is when we stray from the first great commandment of loving God.

This disrespect for ourselves can manifest itself in what can be described as diminishing ways. When we don't believe that we are good and beautiful we try to get our identity by comparing ourselves to others. When we try to get our identity in this way everybody else can become our competitor. We compare ourselves to others to find out who we are. We are only happy with the answer if we believe we are better than those to whom we compared ourselves. Competition, while it can be a great motivator in certain places, can diminish human beings. We see the result of competition so often between countries and religions and organizations, and even within families. It can be very destructive.

When we don't love God as God, when we desire to be God, and when we compete with others in being God, we create a model of society that is based on the concept of a pyramid. In the pyramid model, to be successful, good and beautiful we need to be at the top. There is a problem, however, because as we make our way to the top the space we have to work in gets smaller and smaller and smaller. Therefore, when I move up I have to knock somebody down to make space for me. I have to become more and more powerful. My aim is to get to the top of the pyramid. Then I will have arrived. This attitude is a fruit of not allowing God to be God. It is a destructive way to live. It is a diminishing way to live. It is a way of living that ultimately will not bear fruit. We learn this from what happened to Adam.

After Adam had eaten from the tree of knowledge God was looking for him. God still wanted to be in relationship with Adam. When God found Adam, Adam said to God:

I was afraid because I was naked, so I hid.
(Gen. 3:10)

When Adam ate from the tree of all knowledge, when he tried to be God, rather than love God, he was not satisfied. The knowledge revealed to him who he was. He saw himself in his nakedness. He could not cope with the reality of who he was so he hid. Often sin—rejecting or at least losing contact with who we are and whose we are—leads us to hide. We hide from ourselves. We hide from God. The sacrament of Reconciliation takes us out of hiding. It gives us the confidence to face ourselves and reclaim our identity.

When we love the Lord our God with all our hearts, with all our souls, with all our minds and with all our strength, the pyramid model of society is no longer a model with which we can comfortably work. Loving God enables us to take our place not in the pyramid with everybody as a competitor but in a body with everyone as a sister or brother. Jesus, when he washed his disciples' feet at the Last Supper, inaugurated the body as his model of society rather than a pyramid. Jean Vanier, discussing this, says:

All groups, all societies, are built on the model of the pyramid:

At the top are the powerful, the rich, the intelligent. They are called to govern and guide.

At the bottom are the immigrants, the slaves, the servants, people who are out of work, or who have a mental illness or different forms of disabilities.

They are excluded, marginalized.

Here, Jesus is taking the place of a person at the bottom, the last place, the place of a slave. For Peter this is impossible. Little does he realize that Jesus came to transform the model of society from a pyramid to a body, where each and every person has a place, whatever their abilities and disabilities, where each one is dependent upon the other. Each is called to fulfill a mission in the body of humanity and of the Church. There is no "last place."[21]

This whole idea of the body is a very different model to the pyramid. There is no part of our body that we would want to do without. Each part is necessary for the good of the body. No part of the body is in competition with another part. St. Paul, in his first letter to the Corinthians, uses the analogy of the body to describe our life in God— our life in Jesus. Using the analogy of the body, St. Paul reveals how we live in love with God:

Just as the human body, though it is made up of many parts, is a single unit because all these parts,

21. Jean Vanier, *Drawn into the Mystery of Jesus through the Gospel of John* (London: Darton, Longman and Todd, 2004), 227.

though many, make one body, so it is with Christ. In the one Spirit we were all baptized, Jews as well as Greeks, slaves as well as citizens, and one Spirit was given to us all to drink.

Nor is the body to be identified with any one of its many parts. If the foot were to say, "I am not a hand and so I do not belong to the body," would that mean that it stopped being part of the body? If the ear were to say, "I am not an eye, and so I do not belong to the body," would that mean that it was not a part of the body? If your whole body was just one eye, how would you hear anything? If it was just one ear, how would you smell anything?

Instead of that, God put all the separate parts into the body on purpose. If all the parts were the same, how could it be a body? As it is, the parts are many but the body is one. The eye cannot say to the hand, "I do not need you," nor can the head say to the feet, "I do not need you."

(1 Cor. 12:12–21)

Through our baptism we become part of the body of Christ. It is in Christ's body that we live our love for God. That body is a sacred body and St. Paul also reveals how we are to treat the body:

What is more, it is precisely the parts of the body that seem to be the weakest that are the indispensable ones; and it is the least honorable parts of the body that we clothe with the greatest care. So our more improper parts get decorated in a way that our more proper parts do not need. God has arranged the body so that more dignity is given to the parts which are without it, and so that there may not be disagreements inside the body, but that each part may be equally concerned for all the others. If one part is hurt, all parts are hurt with it. If one part is given special honor, all parts enjoy it.

(1 Cor. 12:22–26)

This brings us to the second great commandment of love—loving our neighbor as ourselves. This also brings us to the second great sin—the sin of the Innkeeper.

WHAT WAS THE SIN OF THE INNKEEPER?

The sin of the Innkeeper is the sin of not having space for the poor and those who are in need. The Innkeeper in Bethlehem on the night that Jesus was born was unable to take in a heavily pregnant woman. He was unable to give her a place to rest. He was unable to facilitate the emergence of life. The Innkeeper was blind to the needs of this woman. He was unable to love his neighbor in a real and practical way. When we love our neighbor we, in fact, love our God. It is impossible to love our neighbor and not love our God just as it is impossible to truly love our God without loving our neighbor. When Jesus spoke about the last judgment he said that whatever we do to the poor and needy we do to him (Mt. 26:40). Jesus identifies himself completely with the poor and needy. He identifies himself with those who are sick, those who are hungry, those who are thirsty, those who are in prison, those who are excluded. If we use the pyramid image of society Jesus is very clearly at the bottom. It is his presence at the bottom of the pyramid that brings dignity to those at the bottom. It is his presence at the bottom that turns the pyramid on its head and allows the body to emerge. The body of Christ is a community of people in relationship. It is a community of love.

Being faithful to the great commandments of love naturally creates a community of love and peace. In this community we are accountable to one another. Fr. Peter McVerry, SJ, when speaking about the sacrament of Reconciliation, says that this sacrament

> is the request to the community for forgiveness from someone who has offended another within the community.[22]

People may object to this definition, saying that it excludes God completely. However, this is not true if we really believe that Jesus is alive and active in the poor and needy. At the heart of the community of love in the body of Christ is the poor. The poor are the royal members of God's kingdom. Our greatest sin arises when we exclude them and refuse to show compassion

22. Peter McVerry, SJ, *Jesus: Social Revolutionary?* (Dublin: Veritas, 2008), 123.

to them in our kingdoms—the kingdoms that we build, but that cannot last. Exclusion of the poor is the sin that Jesus speaks about most. It goes totally against the compassion of God—the Father who waits for and loves his broken son in his fragility. It also goes totally against the mission of Jesus, which is primarily to bring the Good News to the poor. When Fr. Peter McVerry is discussing God he says:

> God is compassion. So what better way of revealing that God is compassion than by ushering into the Kingdom all those who were made to suffer here on earth, all those who were unwanted, rejected, cast out, despised. They enter the Kingdom of God, not because they lived better lives than the rest of us, not because they were more moral than the rest of us—but because God is compassion.
>
> And the rest of us? We will be left scratching our heads and wondering if we, too, might get in. We will get in if we have made friends with the poor. If we have reached out to the poor and tried to relieve their pain, then they will turn around and invite us into *their* Kingdom. If we have simply ignored the poor, then how can we expect them to invite us into their Kingdom? They will— through forgiveness.[23]

23. Ibid., 43.

This reveals in a very powerful way why we celebrate the sacrament of Reconciliation in the community. There is no such thing as a private sin. When we sin we need to be reconciled—we need to be forgiven by God, alive and active in the community. We need to be forgiven by God, alive and active in those who are poor. This is a tremendously humbling reality. In the sacrament of Reconciliation our humble and poor God forgives us. That forgiveness is expressed through a weak and vulnerable community. It is expressed through a weak and vulnerable person who is the ordained leader of the community. When this happens we rediscover who we are and whose we are.

Sometimes the weak and vulnerable ordained leader, the priest, can be a stumbling block to people. Some people find it very difficult to confess their sinfulness to another human being. It is true that it takes great humility to articulate one's sinfulness to another. It is amazing to think that in the early church people confessed their sins publicly! One person in the modern era who continued with this approach was a former Benedictine abbot, Alfred Koch, who every Ash Wednesday

> [I]n the presence of the whole community, with patent meekness and humility admitted his failings of the previous year.[24]

---

24. Rembrandt Weakland, *A Pilgrim in a Pilgrim Church* (Michigan: William B. Eerdmans, 2009), 3.

One very profound public act of confession and repentance took place in Milwaukee in May 2002. There in the Cathedral, Archbishop Rembrandt Weakland, in his last act as archbishop apologized and asked forgiveness from the people he had shepherded for twenty-five years for an inappropriate relationship he'd had with a man shortly after he was made archbishop. It was a most humble and honest thing to do. In his confession the archbishop acknowledged the effect of what he had done on the body of Christ—the community. He said:

> Long ago I placed that sinfulness in God's loving and forgiving heart, but now and into the future I worry about those whose faith may be shaken by my acts.[25]

Here was a man standing in front of his community and confessing his sin and asking for forgiveness. Archbishop Weakland also said:

> The early church was wise to declare that God can use imperfect instruments to build the Kingdom and that the effectiveness of the sacraments does not depend on the holiness of the minister.[26]

The priest in the sacrament of Reconciliation is an imperfect instrument used by God to build up the Kingdom. To consider the role of the priest in the

25. Ibid., 4.
26. Ibid., 3.

sacrament of Reconciliation it can be helpful to think
about Naaman the leper (1 Kings 5:1–14). Naaman
was an important man. When he went to Israel to be
cured of his leprosy he felt insulted. When Elisha the
prophet did not come out and personally greet him he
was offended. Then when he was told to bathe seven
times in the Jordan he was horrified. He protested that
he was quite sure there were superior rivers in his own
country. Yet in all these unexpected and humiliating cir-
cumstances Naaman was healed. Perhaps many of the
objections that people have about confessing to a priest
are as real and as accurate as Naaman's objection. Yet,
for whatever reason, God chooses what is imperfect to
communicate his compassion and forgiveness—to communicate who we are and whose we are.

The imperfect priest, as the ordained leader of the
community, is the one that God has chosen to communicate his forgiveness and compassion in the sacrament of
Reconciliation. So how is God's forgiveness, compassion, commitment and confidence communicated in
the sacrament of Reconciliation?

Sometimes when we start to look at the celebration
of a sacrament we can forget that we are still looking at
a personal relationship and a profound communication
between a lover and the beloved—between a parent
and a child. This profound communication always
takes place in the context of a loving and life giving
family. One of the most beautiful and simple ways of

experiencing this reality is through the eyes of those with learning disabilities—the prophets in our midst. The understanding of the sacraments by people with learning disabilities was discovered by Père Thomas Philippe, the spiritual guide of Jean Vanier. Père Thomas, we are told, discovered that

> disabled people were particularly sensible to the presence of Jesus in the sacraments. They came to the confessional not because of a sense of wrong-doing but because they felt sad. They might not have a very developed sense of sin but they knew the inner turbulence and pain that was counter to the peace of communion, the peace to which Jesus referred when he said "my peace I give unto you." In the vision of Père Thomas therefore, they had a better understanding of the true nature of the sacrament of Reconciliation: the gift of peace by means of which Jesus restored them to the way of faith.[27]

Ultimately, this is the gift of God in the sacrament of Reconciliation—a meeting with Jesus that gives us peace. All that happens in the sacrament communicates God's peace.

27. Kathryn Spink, *The Miracle, the Message, the Story* (London: Darton, Longman and Todd, 2006), 77.

THE SACRAMENT

THE SACRAMENT OF RECONCILIATION IS GOD'S gift to us to express God's humble forgiveness and his confidence in us. The sacrament is the action of God. In the sacrament we are called to respond to God's belief and trust in us by confessing our sins, humbly accepting God's forgiveness and being committed to living as God calls us to live. It is through the power of God's forgiveness that we can leave the sacrament with a firm purpose of amendment. In other words through the power of God's forgiveness we can be truly transformed. Through the action of God and through our own sorrow for our sins we can experience deep conversion. The inner conversion of heart includes sorrow for sin and the intent to lead a new life.[28]

There are four elements to the celebration of the sacrament of Reconciliation. Each of these elements reveals something about our friendship with God and God's commitment to us. The Church tells us that in any teaching about the sacrament, emphasis must be put on God's faithful love and God's mercy for God's people. The ultimate purpose of the sacrament is that we should love God deeply and commit ourselves

28. *Rite of Penance* (Dublin: Veritas, 1976), no. 6.

completely to God (*Rite of Penance*, no. 5). In the sacrament we are inspired to do this through listening to the Word of God. The sacrament expresses the tender and compassionate, forgiving Word of God. Through the Word of God light is received to recognize our sins and the call to conversion and to confidence in God's mercy (*Rite of Penance*, no. 17). The sacrament bears real fruit in our lives when we are "moved to more fervent service of God and neighbor" (*Rite of Penance*, no. 7b).

When we celebrate the sacrament of Reconciliation we are praying. Our prayer is not a private prayer—it is a prayer of the community. This expresses beautifully the communal nature of the sacrament. No matter how confidential the content of the sacrament it is never private. By its very nature, the sacrament of Reconciliation is in itself a communal event. Reconciliation with God is at the same time reconciliation with the Church (*Rite of Penance*, no. 4).

Since it is a prayer, it contains an expression of the faith of the Church, an act of worship and praise of the healing, forgiving love and mercy of God, and a relationship in which the initiative of God and the free response of the human person are manifest (*Rite of Penance*, no. 3).

When we celebrate the sacrament we share in the Paschal Mystery, the life, death, and resurrection of Jesus. That means that it is a renewal of our baptismal commitment and is completed and fulfilled in the Eucharist (*Rite of Penance*, no. 7d & no. 6b).

God's Invitation

The sacrament is God's gift to us; therefore, when we open ourselves to celebrating the sacrament we are responding to an invitation from God—a humble invitation. When we respond to that invitation we are listening to God present in the sanctuary of our lives, in that real fair land—our conscience.

The celebration of the sacrament begins with a welcome. The joy of God needs to be experienced in that welcome. When we go to celebrate the sacrament of Reconciliation we are accepting God's gift. This brings God deep joy. When we enter into the sacrament of Reconciliation we enter into the embrace of the father in the story of the prodigal son. It is as intimate and as tender as that.

At the beginning of the sacrament we need to hear again God's love for his people and his commitment to us.

That happens if we hear the Word of God proclaimed. It is wonderful at the beginning of the sacrament to hear about the covenant that God has made with us. This covenant is God's promise never, ever to abandon us. It is the proclamation of the father who waits for his child to come home. It is the declaration of love made by a lover for their beloved. God desires that we belong in relationship with him always—that we belong in his family. God desires that we make our home in him.

Perhaps the celebration of the sacrament can begin with listening to the Word from the book of the prophet Isaiah:

> Can a mother forget her baby at the breast, or fail to cherish the child of her womb? Yet even if these forget, I will never forget you.
>
> *(Isa. 49:15)*

or

> Do not be afraid, I have redeemed you. I have called you by your name; you are mine. You are precious in my eyes. You are honored and I love you. Do not be afraid, I am with you.
>
> *(Isa. 43:1–4)*

The beginning of the celebration of the sacrament, then, reveals God's love for us, his ongoing commitment to us and that tremendous trust that he has in us by giving us the freedom to accept his gift of forgiveness or not. This sacrament certainly expresses the gift of freedom that we have as children of God. When we celebrate the sacrament we are freely choosing heaven. We are freely choosing to live in friendship with Jesus. In the sacrament we are freed to love. We are liberated and we find peace.

CONTRITION

As we begin the celebration God confesses his love for us. What we confess is our sorrow. For the person going to celebrate the sacrament of Reconciliation one of the primary motivators needs to be true and genuine sorrow. The Church calls this sorrow contrition. Contrition is the first element in the sacrament of Reconciliation. To be contrite is not only an intellectual decision—it is to be sorry at the level of feeling. It is a sorrow that is deeper than anything we can experience in our minds. This sorrow does not emerge solely from an awareness that we have broken a law. It emerges from an awareness that we have caused hurt in a relationship. Therefore, to be sorry demands great humility. To be truly sorry means that you take real responsibility for what you have done or failed to do. This can be very difficult. It can be very difficult to admit that you did something wrong without making some excuse for it. It can be very difficult to admit that your words, your actions or indeed your lack of words or actions have hurt Jesus. Often it is easier to make an excuse rather than accept responsibility. However, contrition for our sins comes from the decision to humbly accept responsibility and become more aware of the humble love of Jesus. Maybe the ultimate experience of contrition is purgatory. Perhaps purgatory is the process that we may have to go through when we wake after death to grow in humility by becoming aware of our sins and also aware of the mercy and love of God for us in our beauty and sinfulness—in the whole truth of our lives. In that humbling awareness, our desire for God will grow and grow until ultimately God will burst through and our desire will be satisfied forever.

Perhaps the greatest example of contrition in the gospel can be found in Peter. During the drama after the Last Supper, Peter denied Jesus. This is at the heart of sin: to deny Jesus; to deny being in friendship with Jesus; to deny knowing Jesus. After this denial, after this sin—the sin of not having space for Jesus; the sin of the innkeeper—Peter had the humility to be so sorry. He was so full of contrition that he wept bitterly. Peter was not weeping because he broke a law or even ignored or denied a law. Peter wept bitterly because he had denied his friend. This was a deep, deep sorrow.

Perhaps in the celebration of the sacrament of Reconciliation this contrition or deep sorrow can be absent. When we celebrate the sacrament out of habit we may focus more on breaking a law than on denying a friend. When we commit a sin regularly we can use the sacrament of Reconciliation to ease momentarily our guilt rather than transform our lives. To illustrate this point starkly: One day in discussion with another person about the issue of child abuse by priests, the other person said that one of the problems must have been that the priests who abused did not go to Confession. I thought a lot about this and then said that I believed that one of the problems was that they did go to Confession and go reg-ularly. The act of the sacrament, they may have believed, released them from the sin of past abusing and freed them sadly to abuse again. This terrible cycle could continue. At no time in this cycle does the one who abuses have to take responsibility for their actions. They can blame a weakness in their character or something outside of themselves for what they do. It is possible to confess a sin without taking any responsibility for that sin or indeed without allowing oneself to become aware of the devastation that the sin caused others.

The same could happen with the man who is an alcoholic. When he is drunk he hits his wife. In Confession he expresses sorrow for what he has done. However he doesn't blame himself. He blames the drink. Then Confession releases him from the guilt and the drink allows him not to blame himself.

There is something wrong with our understanding of the sacrament of Reconciliation when this happens, not only in these dramatic cases but also with our everyday habitual sins. The sacrament of Reconciliation should never be used as something to ease our guilt while leaving our lives untransformed. How could this possibly happen? Perhaps it could happen through a lack of contrition.

The one who uses the sacrament to ease his/her guilt yet carries on untransformed is unlike Peter: he/she has never wept bitterly. That God forgives us in the sacrament is beyond doubt, but to accept that gift of forgiveness, which leads to transformation, we need to weep bitterly. The source of the weeping is not an awareness that we are bad. It is not from an awareness that we have broken a law.

The weeping comes from an awareness that we have damaged or denied our friendship with Jesus. When we take responsibility for that, like Peter, we can be overwhelmed with sadness. It is remarkable that Peter blamed nobody when that cock crowed. He didn't blame the girl who asked him the question. He didn't say that he was afraid. He didn't say that the situation was too pressurized for him to think straight. He didn't even say that he didn't mean it. He just wept bitterly. That is true contrition and that is necessary to be open to accepting the forgiveness of God that God has already freely given.

In the sacrament we express our contrition when we pray our act of contrition. This prayer puts into word our deep sorrow. A particularly beautiful act of contrition comes from St. Alphonsus Liguori:

> I love you, Jesus, my Love above all things. I repent with my whole heart for ever having offended you. Never permit me to separate myself from you again. Grant that I may love you always. Then do with me what you will.

When we are not opened by contrition we are closed to accepting forgiveness. It is when we accept the gift of forgiveness that our lives are transformed.

CONFESSION

Confession is an integral part of accepting the gift of forgiveness. This is a reality with which many of us struggle. We simply don't like to confess. Not many of us are like Abbot Koch, the abbot who confessed his sins publicly to his community each year. We question why we should tell others about our sins. Indeed, if God knows everything, why should there be a need for us to confess? Sometimes, in an incomplete celebration of the sacrament, people are invited not to name any specific sin but just to admit that they are sinners. While the motivation for this may be pastoral kindness to make the sacrament easier for people, sadly I think that it misses a wonderful opportunity for freedom. Naming reality can free us so much. When we deny reality or are afraid to name it we become imprisoned by it. What stops us from naming negative reality about our lives? It may be shame and embarrassment. It may be an inability to accept that we are both beautiful and broken. When we don't name reality it is easier not to take responsibility for it. The ironic thing is that psychologists always encourage people to name reality to enable them to face that reality. People pay a lot of money to do this in therapy. Yet, we struggle often to name reality in that very place where we can receive the power to be freed from what imprisons us—the sacrament of Reconciliation.

Where in the scripture do we have evidence of confession? Who confesses? I think that, again, if we look at Peter we can find the evidence that we need. Peter denied Jesus. He wept bitterly. Then Jesus was crucified. For three days he lay in the tomb and then he rose again. I wonder how Peter was feeling during those days. I'm sure he was feeling bereaved, deep in grief. His bereavement and grief, however, had a sharper pain than that of the others because just before Jesus died Peter disowned him. He must have felt so angry and ashamed of himself. I'm sure he thought, "If only I could turn back the clock!" It must have been awful for Peter to realize that the last thing he did for Jesus before he died was to deny him.

Then came the resurrection. In the gospel of St. John, Peter and John found the tomb empty on that morning. We are told that John saw this and he believed (John 20:8). We are not told whether Peter believed or not. Then, in the evening of that same day, the disciples were behind closed doors in fear. Jesus came and stood in the midst of them. What happened then was amazing. Jesus gave his disciples the gift of peace. Then he sent them out, filled with the Holy Spirit, to be people with the power to forgive sins (John 20:19–23).

Peter was present in this room. Jesus did not address Peter separately. He did not take him to one side and have it out with him about his denial. He did not mention what Peter did. Instead he commissioned Peter, just like all the others, to go out and forgive. In this action Jesus had totally forgiven Peter. This action reveals that Jesus still had complete trust in Peter. I wonder how Peter felt at this meeting. He must have at least felt awkward. He probably felt deeply embarrassed and ashamed. I wonder did he hide at the back of the group or maybe he wondered did Jesus see him at all. In many ways it would have been easier for Peter if Jesus had challenged him and berated him for his denials—but nothing was said. This must have been very difficult for Peter. He must have worried about his relationship with Jesus.

The next time that Peter and Jesus meet, in the gospel of St. John, is at the Sea of Galilee (John 21:1–19). Peter was out fishing with some of the disciples. While they are fishing Jesus shouted to them from the shore. When Peter realized that it was Jesus, he did a very strange and seemingly unnecessary thing. He wrapped a towel around himself and he jumped into the water and went to Jesus. This was strange and seemingly unnecessary because the boat was a hundred yards from land. The question is why did Peter run ahead of the others to Jesus? Perhaps this was the moment of confession. Yes, Jesus had forgiven Peter from the start but Peter still needed to confess. When Peter saw his opportunity to have a short time with Jesus on his own he jumped from the boat and rushed to Jesus. I am convinced that Peter needed to say to Jesus, "Do you know that I denied you and that I am sorry?" This is what happens when we confess in the sacrament of Reconciliation. We make eye contact with Jesus. We tell him the truth and we ask him if we are okay. To accept the gift of forgiveness we really need to confess.

Just as Jesus did not tell the other disciples the content of the conversation he had with Peter on the shore at Galilee, when we confess in the sacrament of Reconciliation what we say remains forever between us and Jesus. The confidence of Jesus is expressed through the actions of the priest. This sacred confidentiality is described using the term the "Seal of Confession." This seal is vital in the sacrament because what is being articulated in the sacrament is a conversation between Jesus and the person confessing. If the person confessing is truly contrite and has humbly accepted the gift of forgiveness he/she will take responsibility for the actions that he/she confessed. Taking this responsibility is concretely expressed when they take whatever action is necessary, painful as that may be, to do what is right. The sacrament of Reconciliation can never be an easy way to admit your faults and be released from them without ever taking responsibility for them. The person who confesses cannot hide behind the Seal of Confession. It is their responsibility to allow the power of forgiveness to give them the courage they need to face up to the reality of their lives in whatever way necessary.

ABSOLUTION

What is God's response to our contrition and our confession? Forgiveness! That's it. Nothing more and nothing less. God forgives us. He looks at us and his eyes are not eyes of disappointment or anger—they are eyes of compassion and love. God's expression of forgiveness is so powerful. That power is not manifest in any magical way; it is manifest in a very real way. The real way that it is manifest is by enabling us to take our normal place in the community again. When we accept the forgiveness of God we are at home again in the community which is the Body of Christ.

We find evidence of this in the story of Peter. As soon as Peter had his conversation with Jesus he immediately returned to the other disciples. He pulled the nets full of fish onto the shore and then he shared a meal with Jesus. For Peter, I have no doubt, the meal was a celebration of a reconciliation that had been completed. Peter confessed and then Jesus probably looked at him in the eye and said, "Peter, you are forgiven." Then they probably embraced before Peter went back to the others. The moment of forgiveness is the moment of embrace. It is that moment when that sanctuary, which is that place within us where we are at one with God, encompasses our whole being.

The moment of forgiveness or the embrace of God is celebrated in the sacrament of Reconciliation in absolution. Absolution is a most profound act. It is an act of tremendous humility. God humbly confesses his confidence and trust in us and we humbly accept his forgiveness. God makes his confession through the priest. Accepting this forgiveness through the priest is an act of humility towards the Church and the priest.

Absolution has three elements. The first is the imposition of hands. Laying on of hands is central in the sacramental rite. This ritual symbolizes the reality that God's forgiveness comes through the Church and human acceptance.[29] It also signifies our participation in the communion of the Holy Spirit (*CCC*, 699). This developed in the early church, where the imposition of hands in reconciliation was closely connected with the action of the Holy Spirit in the community.[30] The Holy Spirit directed the community in all things. In the Gospels Jesus heals the sick and blesses little children by laying hands on them (Mk. 10:13–16). The imposition of hands should be done in silence for a few moments before and after the words of absolution.

The second element of absolution is the formula that is used. This emphasizes the fact that forgiveness comes from the mercy of the Father, through the death and resurrection of his Son, made known through the Spirit. This forgiveness is prayed in and through the Church.

The third element of absolution is the tracing of the sign of the cross over the penitent. This is a sign that the person is baptized and that that commitment is renewed or deepened.

> God uses visible signs to give salvation and to renew the broken covenant.
>
> (Rite of Penance, *no. 6d*)

29. James Dallen, *The Reconciling Community: The Rite of Penance* (Collegeville, Minnesota: The Liturgical Press, 1986), 335.
30. Ibid., 359.

Through the gift of absolution the person who is contrite and has confessed is empowered to reclaim their friendship with Jesus. Evidence of this reconciliation is found in the transformation of the person's life. This transformation is manifest in acts of penance or satisfaction. Reconciliation is celebrated when the community celebrates the Eucharist. Evidence of this is found when Peter had the meal with Jesus and the other disciples on the shore at Galilee. There Jesus broke the bread. They shared in the one bread. The disciples with Peter shared in the life of Jesus.

Today we express the culmination of reconciliation when we celebrate the Eucharist. Reconciliation leads us to the table of the Eucharist. There we share in the life of Jesus when we share in his sacrifice. We are sinners who have humbly accepted the gift of forgiveness through our contrition and confession. Now, as sinners at peace with God, we share in the one chalice of blood that is poured out for the forgiveness of sins. The new and everlasting covenant is about sin and forgiveness.

Take this, all of you, and drink from it:
for this is the chalice of my blood,
the blood of the new and eternal covenant. It
will be poured out for you and for many for
the forgiveness of sins.
Do this in memory of me.

By drinking from the chalice we acknowledge that we are sinners who receive the gift of forgiveness. We also witness to the fact that we are members of the new covenant—that we really are sharers in the life of Jesus. As sharers in the life of Jesus we are called to continue the mission of Jesus on earth. We are called to be the presence of Jesus on earth. We do that by being reconcilers ourselves.

ACTS OF PENANCE (SATISFACTION)

The gift of the sacrament of Reconciliation, then, is not an end in itself. It leads to the Eucharist. It leads to Holy Communion. It leads to a transformation of life. This transformation of life is explained in the introduction to the Rite:

> Freed from sin by the grace of Christ they may work with all people of good will for justice and peace in the world.
>
> (Rite of Penance, no. 5)

How does this actually take place? How does this happen? Again to answer these questions we return to Peter on the shore at Galilee (John 21:15–19). When they had finished the meal Jesus asked Peter three times, "Do you love me?" Peter got annoyed that he was asked three times but each time that Peter answered, Jesus asked him to feed his lambs and to feed his sheep. In asking these questions Jesus reveals again that Peter is completely

forgiven and that Jesus is trusting him with his family.
More than that, Jesus is trusting Peter to love his family.
It is a tremendous confidence that Jesus has in Peter. In
fact, Jesus has chosen to depend on Peter to be his love.
Jean Vanier says:

> But Peter can only guide, nourish and be respon-
>> sible for people
> in the name of Jesus *if he loves Jesus*,
> and I dare say *if he loves Jesus*
> *passionately*
> and is prepared to give his life for Jesus.
> We can only assume a responsibility in the name of
> Jesus
> if we love Jesus and become his friend.
> This is not something devotional or sentimental. It
> is a commitment to help people
> to whom we are not especially attracted to
> grow in their love of Jesus
> and to work with them.
> Not seeking to control them but to liberate them.[31]

This is at the heart of satisfaction in the sacrament of
Reconciliation. The Rite of Penance states:

> This act of penance, may suitably take the form
> of prayer, self-denial, and especially service of one's

31. Jean Vanier, *Drawn into the Mystery of Jesus through the Gospel of
John* (London: Darton, Longman and Todd, 2004), 353.

neighbor and works of mercy. These underline the fact that sin and its forgiveness have a social aspect.

(Rite of Penance, *no. 18*)

In our act of penance we take responsibility for loving in the name of Jesus. When we accept the forgiveness of God we are liberated from what is broken in us—from our compulsions—to love in the name of Jesus. The fruit of the sacrament of Reconciliation is seen in how we treat our sisters and brothers in humanity. In the sacrament, God expresses his trust and his confidence in us again. In the sacrament God also reveals that he depends on us to be the love of Jesus. We accept his confidence, his trust and, indeed, his dependence when we love others in the name of his Son, when we commit ourselves to them, when we work with them, when we liberate them, and when we passionately love Jesus.

CELEBRATING THE SACRAMENT

S O HOW DO WE CELEBRATE THIS GIFT OF RECONCILIATION? How do we look God in the eye honestly and see his loving eyes looking back? How do we accept God's confession of love, belief and forgiveness? The simplest answer is to take courage and go to Confession! Be contrite; weep bitterly for your sins; weep bitterly that at times you want to be God, at times you have no space for Jesus. Confess your sins openly and humbly without excuse. Take responsibility for them. Have the humility to accept the humble forgiveness of God. Love in his name.

How often should you do this and where should you do this? It is good to celebrate the sacrament of Reconciliation regularly—perhaps every two months. It is also good to celebrate it before big occasions—Easter, Christmas, Marriage, Confirmation, birthdays, anniversaries and holidays.

How should you celebrate the sacrament of Reconciliation? It is good that the parish comes together from time to time to celebrate reconciliation. This reveals the communal nature of sin and the fact that forgiveness is communicated by God through his Body, the Church. There is no such thing as a private sin and there is no such thing as private absolution. Every sin we commit affects the community and it is God through the Church, in the person of the priest, who absolves. In many parishes before Christmas and Easter there are Penitential Services. These Penitential Services can be very powerful when you witness so many people celebrating the sacrament of Reconciliation—when you witness so many people confessing their sins and being forgiven. It can be a transforming moment for a parish. This moment can be extended if the parish was to organize a week of reconciliation. Such weeks would begin on a Sunday assembly and culminate the following Sunday in the sharing of the chalice at the Eucharistic celebration. Between the two Sundays certain tasks would be carried out. There would be prayer and reflection during this week which would take place in the home. The family could gather for scripture reading that would allow for reflection on the mercy and forgiveness of God. The psalms could also be prayed. Reflection on personal experiences of reconciliation would also be encouraged. During the week there would be a Penitential Service in the church. All other parish activities would be suspended for the week. Imagine the joy at the Sunday Eucharist if the whole parish, for the previous week, focused on the sacrament of Reconciliation.[32]

32. See Mary Collins, OSB, "Festivals 6f Reconciliation," in *The Echo Within, Emerging Issues in Religious Education*, ed. C. Dooley and M. Collins (Allen, Texas: Thomas More Publishing, 1997), 71–85.

If we are celebrating the sacrament outside an orga-
nized parish celebration I think that time should be made
to plan the celebration. It may not be a good idea to rush
into a church and get Confession. If it is possible it may
be better to go to celebrate the sacrament with a friend
or as a family. If time permits (perhaps time should be
created to permit) a day or half a day could be set aside.
The day could begin with a walk. Then the sacrament
is celebrated and then a meal is shared to celebrate
the gift received. In doing this the time becomes a real
celebration. It becomes a public celebration in a sense
and sin and forgiveness are more integrated in our lives.
Celebrating the sacrament should not be a hidden occa-
sion but a time to share joy with others.

Before we celebrate the sacrament it is very important
to take time to visit that real fair land within us. It is necessary to go to the sanctuary within us and examine our
conscience. When we are examining our conscience we
are asking ourselves when have we failed to live the two
great commandments of love—love for God and love for
neighbor. In other words, we are asking ourselves when
we have committed the sin of Adam and Eve, which
breaks the commandment to love God, and when we
have committed the sin of the Innkeeper, which breaks
the commandment to love our neighbor.

Perhaps what can help us in our examination are the
following questions based on the story of the rich young

man who had not the space for Jesus in his life—the rich young man who found his identity in what he owned rather than in God.

Do I trust God's confidence in me?
An examination of conscience

Read the rich young man—Mark 10:17–22

The rich young man knelt before Jesus.
Do I acknowledge Jesus in my life? Do I have space for God?
Do I seek, respect and respond to his Word?

The rich young man wanted to inherit eternal life.
Do I want to be close to Jesus always?
Do I want to do the best I can with the gift of my life? Do I believe that I can accept the gift of heaven by the way I live on earth?

Jesus asked the rich young man did he keep the Ten Commandments.
Do I keep the Ten Commandments?
Do I realize that rather than stopping me doing things they free me to be myself?
Do I respect myself as the beautiful creation that God made me?

Jesus looked steadily at the rich young man and loved him.
Do I believe that Jesus looks at me and loves me?
Do I believe that Jesus invites me to share in his life?
Do I believe that Jesus believes in me?

Jesus told the rich young man to sell everything he had and give the money to the poor.
Do I make space for Jesus in my life through loving and caring for others, especially my family?
Do I recognize the face of Jesus in those who are marginalized, disrespected, those who live in poverty and those who are vulnerable?
Do I recognize everybody in the world as my sister or brother equal in the eyes of God?

Jesus then told the rich young man to follow him.
Do I believe that Jesus has a plan for my life? Do I make an effort to discover that plan? Do I trust Jesus enough to accept his plan?

The rich young man went away sad.
Do I choose the way of Jesus or do my own thing?
Do I accept that sin brings sadness?
Do I accept that true happiness can only be found in Jesus?
In other words, do I allow God to be God in my life and do I welcome Jesus into my life?

It is when we examine our conscience to the best of our ability that we can weep bitterly for our sins and the hurt we have caused to Jesus. Then, like Peter, we will have an absolute need to confess. In the moment of confession the Father's humble wait is over and we enter the forgiving embrace of God. Then we accept God's confession and receive a liberation and freedom to go in peace to love as we are loved.

I realized this so profoundly when I visited the Holy Land with a friend. At the end of praying the Stations of the Cross through the tiny streets of the old city of Jerusalem we arrived at the Church of the Holy Sepulcher.

In it are the sites of the Crucifixion and the Resurrection. Here we were in the holy of holies. So much of our lives and deaths are shaped by what happened in this place. Yet there was something strange about the place. It did not seem to have the intimacy of some of the other places we had visited. Then we met a monk. He was from Argentina. He had a big beard and the most saintly eyes. He had only one arm—his left arm. He was celebrating the sacrament of Reconciliation. Here at the site of the Crucifixion and Resurrection of Jesus we celebrated the forgiveness of God. Then I realized that it was not about the building but about what happened in the building and indeed what continues to happen every time we celebrate the sacrament of Reconciliation. Jesus believes in us. Jesus forgives us. Jesus trusts us. Jesus gives himself for us. Jesus never wants to be separated from us. This is the confession of God. In the Church of the Holy Sepulcher we celebrated Reconciliation where the gentle face and compassionate eyes of Jesus allowed us to see again that we belong in the forgiving heart of God. From there we share the life of Jesus—a life that, despite any and every passion, can always end in the resurrection.

BIBLIOGRAPHY

Beckett, Sr. Wendy, *Sister Wendy on Prayer* (London: Continuum, 2006).

Catechism of the Catholic Church (Dublin: Veritas, 1994).

Cullen, Bill, *Golden Apples* (London: Hodder and Stoughton Ltd., 2005).

Dallen, James, "Sacrament of Reconciliation," in *The New Dictionary of Sacramental Worship*, ed. Peter E. Fink SJ (Dublin: Gill and Macmillan, 1990).

Dallen, James, *The Reconciling Community: The Rite of Penance* (Collegeville, Minnesota: The Liturgical Press, 1986).

Dooley, Catherine, "The Role of the Community in the Sacrament of Reconciliation," *Louvain Studies 14* (1989).

Dooley, C. and Collins, M., *The Echo Within: Emerging Issues in Religious Education* (Allen, Texas: Thomas More Publishing, 1997).

Eliot, T.S., *Four Quartets* (London: Faber and Faber, 2001).

Ilibagiza, Immaculee, *Left to Tell* (California: Hay House, 2006).

Jerusalem Bible (London: Darton, Longman and Todd, 1974).

Macken, Walter, *Seek the Fair Land* (London: Pan Books, 1962).

McVerry, SJ, Peter, *Jesus: Social Revolutionary?* (Dublin: Veritas, 2008).

Newman, John Henry, *Letter to the Duke of Norfolk* (1875).

Pope Benedict XVI, *Pastoral Letter of the Holy Father Pope Benedict XVI to the Catholics of Ireland* (Dublin: Veritas, 2010).

Rite of Penance (Dublin: Veritas, 1976).

Rohr, Richard, *The Naked Now* (New York: Crossroads Publishing Company, 2009).

Rohr, Richard, *Soul Brothers* (New York: Orbis Books, 2004).

Rolheiser, Ronald, "God judges no one," *The Catholic Herald* (25 September 2009).

Second Vatican Council (Dublin: Dominican, 1977).

Spink, Kathryn, *The Miracle, the Message, the Story* (London: Darton, Longman and Todd, 2006).

Vanier, Jean, *Drawn into the Mystery of Jesus through the Gospel of John* (London: Darton, Longman and Todd, 2004).

Vanier, Jean, "Letter of Jean Vanier" (Spring, 2011).

Weakland, Rembrandt, *A Pilgrim in a Pilgrim Church* (Michigan: William B. Eerdmans, 2009).

Williamson, Marianne, "Our Deepest Fear" in *Return to Love: Reflections on the Principles of "A Course in Miracles"* (New York: Harper Collins, 1992).

Woodhouse, Patrick, *Etty Hillesum: A Life Transformed* (London: Continuum, 2009).

ABOUT PARACLETE PRESS

WHO WE ARE

Paraclete Press is a publisher of books, recordings, and DVDs on Christian spirituality. Our publishing represents a full expression of Christian belief and practice—from Catholic to Evangelical, from Protestant to Orthodox.

We are the publishing arm of the Community of Jesus, an ecumenical monastic community in the Benedictine tradition. As such, we are uniquely positioned in the marketplace without connection to a large corporation and with informal relationships to many branches and denominations of faith.

WHAT WE ARE DOING

Books | Paraclete publishes books that show the richness and depth of what it means to be Christian. Although Benedictine spirituality is at the heart of all that we do, we publish books that reflect the Christian experience across many cultures, time periods, and houses of worship. We publish books that nourish the vibrant life of the church and its people—books about spiritual practice, formation, history, ideas, and customs.

We have several different series, including the best-selling Paraclete Essentials and Paraclete Giants series of classic texts in contemporary English; Voices from the Monastery—men and women monastics writing about living a spiritual life today; award-winning poetry; best-selling gift books for children on the occasions of baptism and first communion; and the Active Prayer Series that brings creativity and liveliness to any life of prayer.

Recordings | From Gregorian chant to contemporary American choral works, our music recordings celebrate sacred choral music through the centuries. Paraclete distributes the recordings of the internationally acclaimed choir Gloriæ Dei Cantores, praised for their "rapt and fathomless spiritual intensity" by *American Record Guide*, and the Gloriæ Dei Cantores Schola, which specializes in the study and performance of Gregorian chant. Paraclete is also the exclusive North American distributor of the recordings of the Monastic Choir of St. Peter's Abbey in Solesmes, France, long considered to be a leading authority on Gregorian chant.

Videos | Our videos offer spiritual help, healing, and biblical guidance for life issues: grief and loss, marriage, forgiveness, anger management, facing death, and spiritual formation.

Learn more about us at our website:
www.paracletepress.com, or
call us toll-free at 1-800-451-5006.

SCAN
TO
READ
MORE

Also available from Paraclete Press . . .

CENTERING PRAYERS
A One-Year Daily Companion for Going Deeper into the Love of God
Peter Traben Haas

ISBN: 978-1-61261-415-1
$18.99, Paperback

Centering Prayers is a collection of 365 inspired prayers crafted as brief preludes or postludes to periods of personal, contemplative prayer—each radiating God's love. Tailored for the seasons and months of the year, they integrate a spiritual theology with certain mystical depth.

PRAYER AS NIGHT FALLS
Experiencing Compline
Kenneth V. Peterson

ISBN: 978-1-61261-376-5
$19.99, Paperback with flaps

This comprehensive look at the ever-popular contemplative prayer service of Compline allows you to experience and participate in the last office of the daily cycle of fixed-hour prayer. Kenneth Peterson tells the story of the history and themes of the office, woven together with reflections from his own spiritual journey.

Available from most booksellers or through Paraclete Press:
www.paracletepress.com
1-800-451-5006
Try your local bookstore first.